PLAIN
TALK
ON
James

PLAIN
TALK
ON
James

MANFORD GEORGE GUTZKE
PH.D.

**Lamplighter
Books** Grand Rapids,
Michigan
Zondervan Publishing House

PLAIN TALK ON JAMES
Copyright © 1969 by Zondervan Publishing House
Grand Rapids, Michigan

ISBN 0-310-25561-9

Library of Congress Catalog Card Number: 73-81059

Lamplighter Books are published by Zondervan Publishing House, 1415 Lake Drive,
S.E., Grand Rapids, Michigan 49506

ACKNOWLEDGMENTS

We are grateful for the permission given us to quote from the following Bible translations:

The Amplified New Testament, copyrighted 1958 by the Lockman
Foundation and published by the Zondervan Publishing House,
Grand Rapids, Michigan.

Good News for Modern Man, the Today's English Version of the New
Testament, copyrighted 1966 by the American Bible Society, New
York, New York.

The New English Bible, New Testament. © The Delegates of the Ox-
ford University Press and the Syndics of the Cambridge University
Press 1961.

The New Testament in Modern English, translated by J. B. Phillips,
copyrighted 1958. Reprinted by permission of the Macmillan Company, New York, and Geoffrey Bles, Ltd., London.

Printed in the United States of America

84   85   86   87   88 — 20   19   18

CONTENTS

1. Salutation 9
2. The Function of Temptation 14
3. The Goal of Patience 19
4. Asking for Wisdom 24
5. Loss in Wavering 28
6. The Weakness of the Rich 31
7. Blessing in Endurance 36
8. Desire Causes Temptation 40
9. Good Gifts Are From God 44
10. Hear With Meekness 48
11. Doers Not Hearers 52
12. Pure Religion 56
13. Have No Respect for Persons 61
14. Avoid Favoring the Rich 65
15. The Meaning of the Law 69
16. Faith Without Works Is Dead 73
17. Faith Alone Is Not Valid 77
18. Faith Made Perfect by Works 81
19. Rahab Was Justified 85
20. So Faith Without Works Is Dead 88
21. The Danger in Being a Teacher 92
22. A Little Can Do a Lot 97
23. The Tongue Is Unruly 100
24. Out of the Same Mouth 104
25. A Good Tree Brings Good Fruit 108
26. An Earthly Mind Is Evil 112
27. Wisdom From Above Is Pure 115
28. Origin of War 119
29. Barren Praying 122
30. Friendship With the World 125
31. He Giveth More Grace 128
32. Draw Nigh to God 131
33. Cleanse for Blessing 134

34. Do Not Judge Others 137
35. Do Not Count on Time 139
36. Frailty of Life 142
37. Definition of Sin 145
38. Miseries of the Rich 148
39. Fraud Is Noted by God 151
40. Wicked Have Oppressed 154
41. Patience Waits With Hope 157
42. Patience Awaits the Coming of the Lord 160
43. Grudge Not 164
44. Example of the Prophets 167
45. The Patience of Job 170
46. Remember at All Times 173
47. Prayer for the Sick 176
48. Believing Prayer Will Accomplish 179
49. Pray for One Another 182
50. The Prayer of a Believing Man 186

PLAIN
TALK
ON
James

Chapter 1

SALUTATION

James, a servant of God and of the Lord Jesus Christ, to the twelve tribes which are scattered abroad, greeting (James 1:1).

The Book of James is a practical message to Christians to help them enter into the full blessing of the Gospel. There is no involved argument about any problem of faith, nor is there any one idea to be found in all his comments. James deals with various matters which arise in Christian living, very much like a gardener hoeing weeds or an orchard-keeper pruning his fruit trees. While there seems to be no single line of thought, it is quite obvious in all that James writes that he wants believers to be blessed.

In many respects this book shows the influence of the Old Testament prophets — in figures of speech, in topics of concern and in plain spoken exhortations. While the book's good common sense would make it both interesting and profitable for anyone to read, it is important to remember that James is writing to persons who have received Jesus Christ as Saviour and Lord. He wants them to have the fullest blessing possible through the grace of God in the Lord Jesus Christ.

It is not entirely clear as to who is the author of this short book. In the early church and in the apostolic company there were several men called "James." One of the best known of these was the brother of John. We read again and again of the three disciples: Peter, James and John, who were so close to the Lord Jesus. The brothers, James and John, were the sons of Zebedee. In the book of Acts we read that Herod killed this

James, the brother of John, with the sword. His death occurred before the disciples started their missionary activities. So we may be sure this book was not written by James the brother of John.

Another "James" is mentioned in the first chapter of the book of Acts, "the son of Alphaeus." Again in the fifteenth chapter of Acts there is a record of a man called "James" who seemed to act as moderator of that great council meeting of the church in Jerusalem. In his epistle to the Galatians Paul speaks of having met "James the Lord's brother." This man seemed to be one of the pillars of the church, and so it could very well be that he was the moderator of the church referred to in Acts 15.

The very fact that none of this shows clearly who was the author of this letter, indicates something important. Only in recent times have Bible students raised questions about the authorship of the books of the Bible. The New Testament writers often referred to Old Testament Scriptures by using the names of the authors. Thus they referred to the writings of Moses. They referred to some of the Psalms as the writings of David, and to some of the prophets by name. But there is never any particular interest in the author as a person, as recorded in the New Testament. Neither was any reference ever made to the conditions under which the books were written.

The significance of all this can be felt when it is noted that at no time was there any modification of the meaning, nor any discounting of the emphasis of any book in the Bible, because of the man who wrote it. As a matter of fact no attention was ever given to the authors of the Scriptures nor to the times when any of it was written. It seems to have been very much the same as when we receive an important telegram: we do not normally pay any attention to the messenger who delivered it. I suggest that this is a very fine procedure for us to follow when we read the Bible.

The Bible does not make a comment about the authorship of the Scripture. In the epistle of Peter, we read " . . . holy men of God spake as they were moved by the Holy Spirit" (II Peter 1:21). This whole problem has become serious for Bible study in our times. When we start paying attention to the author of a book and begin to think of the human being who wrote it, we are in danger of encouraging subversive ideas. Soon some people will say that the Bible contains the Word of God. This suggests that some parts of the Bible are not divinely inspired, because they are of human origin, and this gives a wrong impression of the significance of Scripture.

Some will say the Bible should be compared to ore which comes out of the mine and needs to be smelted in the furnace. In this way, they claim, the dross will be burned away and the pure refined gold of the word will remain. And so these men take the Scriptures and begin to "refine" them with critical processes. They profess to be removing all the human elements so that they may get at what they can accept as the Word of God.

Sometimes these scholars use as an illustration a fruit like a banana. They point out that you take off the peel before you eat the banana. In this and other ways they intimate that not every part of the Bible is for our use.

Years ago it was discovered, and I expect now it is widely known, that many essential vitamins are contained in what we call the "peelings" of an Irish potato. Several generations ago it was not uncommon for the crew of a sailing vessel to be stricken by a disease called scurvy. Many men died of this disease. Later it was found, quite by accident, that by throwing away the peelings of fruits and vegetables, many valuable minerals and vitamins had been destroyed, and so the members of the crew were actually suffering because they lacked these very elements in their diet. These sailors need not have died of the scurvy if they had eaten whole potatoes.

There no doubt are many people who develop "spiritual scurvy" because they "peel off" part of the Bible. When they read the Bible and come across something which they do not understand, they are inclined to "peel" that part off. In doing this they fail to realize that all the Bible is for their use. The parts they discard may actually contain valuable "vitamins" needed for their spiritual health and life.

The answer to our earlier question, "Who was this man called James who wrote the general epistle of James?" is actually not a matter of importance to us. It does not really matter who wrote the book. When we take a doctor's prescription to a pharmacy to be filled, it does not matter to us whether we know the name of the druggist who fills it. His name may be Tom, Dick or Harry. All that is important to us is that the prescription be filled and that it contain what is called for by the doctor who wrote it. When we come to the Bible we have in mind that the Holy Spirit wrote the prescription. This is all we need to know.

While this discussion may seem rather figurative, it can help us to understand that our plan will be, as far as we are concerned, to read and study the Book of James, as it is written, even though we are not sure which "James" is the author. Our attitude will be that this book was written for us. It was preserved for us. It comes to us with a message. And we will read it and study it to learn that message as we can.

Now let us look again at the first verse.

> "James, a servant of God and of the Lord Jesus Christ, to the twelve tribes which are scattered abroad, greeting."

The combination of words, "a servant of God and the Lord Jesus Christ" recognizes the Lord Jesus Christ as being equal with God. Note that whereas James used the word "God" without any adjective, in speaking of Christ he uses the whole title — "the Lord Jesus Christ." To have used only the name "Jesus" would have been inadequate. Nowhere in his book does James refer to the Lord by using only the name of "Jesus." This is of course quite proper because at the time that James wrote this book, Jesus had been glorified. When He was glorified He was made Lord. When He entered into the presence of God, He was made Christ. "God made that same Jesus whom you crucified both Lord and Christ" (Acts 2:36, paraphrased). It is worth noticing James gives Him His total title as he addresses his message to the twelve tribes which are scattered abroad.

For many these words, ". . . to the twelve tribes," would indicate that James was writing to the Jews. But James had no reason for writing to the Jewish people. He was not one of their High Priests nor one of their rabbis. The Jews would not have paid attention to his writings for he was a Christian, a minister of the Gospel of Jesus Christ. It would seem that "the twelve tribes scattered" refers, in an idiomatic way, to the people of God, as we might say, "the whole of Christendom." There is actually a real fitness in this very expression, because "the twelve tribes scattered abroad" could mean all the Christians. Acts 8:1 records the fact that after the death of Stephen and the persecution begun by Saul, the Christians were driven out of Jerusalem. They were scattered abroad through many regions.

It will be helpful to keep in mind as we study this book that James is writing to these dispersed, persecuted Christians who believed on the Lord Jesus Christ. He served them by showing them the real plan of the Gospel as it is in Jesus Christ.

Chapter 2

THE FUNCTION OF TEMPTATION

> My brethren, count it all joy when ye fall into divers temptations, Knowing this, that the trying of your faith worketh patience (James 1:2, 3).

Are problems good for a Christian? I can remember in my early years in school how I would think, "Why did the teacher give me a problem I cannot do? If I did not have this problem, I would not make any mistakes."

It is quite true that without the problems there would be no mistakes, but something else is also true. Without the problems which exercised us in spelling and reading and arithmetic and English we would never have learned anything. And this points to something real for the Christian.

No one would ever expect to play the piano without making mistakes. We may be sure that no one ever learned to play the piano who did not make mistakes, and hit the wrong keys. Suppose I say, that since I always make mistakes when I play, I will not practice, what then? Well then of course I will never learn to play. So it is with reference to spiritual things. The Christian actually needs problems to gain wisdom and strength as he lives.

We can see this in trees that grow in the open. Some plants can be raised under hot house conditions, but an oak tree growing in the open field where wind, rain and storms descend on it, becomes strong because of these adverse conditions.

Something like this is possible as far as the life of a Christian is concerned. In the book of James deeper and more spiritual

14

reasons are revealed as being served by Christians having problems, than these examples have indicated.

The epistle of James is quite different in style from the epistles written by Paul or even those written by Peter. In Paul's case there are arguments. In his letters to the churches, he will discuss some topic or some theme and then give proofs to support his explanations. In his pastoral epistles such as Timothy and Titus this approach is not so clearly seen. These letters are more like James, but Paul's major epistles have a characteristic style which is quite his own.

The general epistle of James does not have one single theme. It does not have a plot in its construction. Actually this whole book is like an instruction manual for a gardener. We can begin to read any portion in such a book and find a complete message at that point dealing with some aspect of gardening. This is the style of the epistle of James.

James is actually working to cultivate or culture healthy spiritual life. In the study of this book the reader will find many practical problems that come up in daily Christian living. James will show us what to consider, what decisions to make and what actions to take which will result in healthy spiritual living. There is no build-up throughout the book. Its beginning is not an introduction, and the ending is not a conclusion. There is no argument throughout it. There is no climax in this book. It is easy reading and can be very helpful. By presenting one problem after another and showing the way in which the believer should meet each situation described, a simple, practical and very useful contribution is made to personal spiritual experience.

In the portion contained in these verses, the problem being considered is "temptation." The phrase, "the trying of your faith," is a definition of what is meant by "temptation." Temptation can come to us in many various ways. We think of being tempted because of our desires and because of the attractiveness of something that we want to have for ourselves. But the believer may also be tempted or tested when he finds himself under severe strain. This is often illustrated in any store. A woman comes in to buy cloth. It need not be expensive cloth but she wants it to be stout enough to stand a certain amount of strain. So while she is in the store, the clerk shows her a piece of goods, and she pulls on it. She takes it in her hand and she pulls it this way, and that, to see if it will take the proper amount of strain. She is making sure that it is right for her purpose. That's testing it.

A man may come to the store to buy a saw or a tool of some kind. He may want to try it out. He will "test" it to see how it stands up under the strain and pressure he is expecting to put on it. This is "testing" or "temptations" as James sees it.

> My brethren, count it all joy when ye fall into divers temptations; Knowing this, that the trying of your faith worketh patience (James 1:2, 3).

In Romans 5:3, 4 Paul wrote: "We glory in tribulations also, knowing that tribulation worketh patience. . . . " This is the same idea. "Tribulation" and "the trying of your faith" are experiences which produce the same results. When we say that tribulation worketh patience we mean it results in, it works it out, that we have patience. This is what James is saying in his discussion at this point.

In studying his statement, much may be learned by noting the particular words and phrases which he uses. "Count it all joy, when you fall into divers temptations." The word "divers" means "various kinds." Diverse would be another way of saying it. Temptations come in different ways. A man may find himself in a situation where his faith is put under severe strain because of a physical condition. He may be feeling ill all day because of a headache or stomach trouble, either of which could be a real handicap. He may find that his assurance of God's blessing is affected and his faith is sorely tried. He did believe in God, but there he is in physical trouble. This could be a real test of his confidence in God, a trying of his faith.

Sometimes a man's faith is put to the test when he has domestic problems. His children may want something he cannot give them. Strain may follow where there is a difference of opinion between husband and wife. Differences between people living in the same house may also become a trial of our faith. Christians want to be patient and kind and gentle. They would like to be considerate of other people but some folks are just downright provoking. This can be a sore trial to the disposition of the believer who wants to show goodwill toward them.

Sometimes the temptation is financial. A Christian may overspend and run short of money and run into debt. In such a case money worries could actually incline a man away from God. They could try his faith.

Sometimes the testing of faith may be social. A Christian might be shunted off to one side and overlooked in the consideration for some position or some particular privilege. This could be a definite testing along several lines.

The trying of a Christian's faith may occur in still other ways. A Christian may for instance be depending for his living on the wages he receives. Then his employer adopts a policy with which he cannot agree. He thinks that the action which has been taken is wrong. He feels dissatisfaction with the whole procedure. He may disapprove this policy because he thinks his Lord will disapprove. He may show his disapproval in all honesty. In such a situation this man could lose his job. The office manager or foreman may not want him around. Either may seek any kind of reason to find fault with him and fire him. So this man faces a real problem. This is a "trying of his faith."

Sometimes a Christian finds himself in a situation where he may be offered a contract if he is willing to compromise his testimony by doing what he feels is wrong. If he will not compromise he will lose the contract. This would be "trying his faith."

Each one of these trials "worketh patience." It produces by such experience of believing and trusting a certain toughness in the Christian faith. A Christian will keep on believing in spite of all that may happen. He will have the disposition to persist.

"Patience" is not so much a matter of being quiet and long suffering in any given situation. It is more a matter of seeing things through. It is that the Christian will keep on keeping on. His faith becomes strong and unwavering as he puts it into practice day after day as he faces the problems of living. As a matter of fact, without problems a Christian would not have the opportunity to exercise his faith over and over again in this way.

For this reason James says, "Count it all joy" even if the going is rough. Eventually the Christian will find that all things will work together for good by the grace of God. He will find renewed strength, trusting in God. He can understand that all such experiences are intended to develop him in the Lord.

Chapter 3

THE GOAL OF PATIENCE

But let patience have her perfect work, that ye may be perfect
and entire, wanting nothing (James 1:4).

In reading the book of James we feel it is as though we were
being advised how to prune a shrub. Taking our shears we go
out and snip off this twig and that twig, and this branch and
that branch. We keep on trimming. This trimming is done
either for appearance or, in the case of pruning, to develop and
improve the fruit-bearing value. We cut off the dead material
and trim out the excess branches. In this way we prepare it
so that it will bear better fruit. We cut these branches one
by one. Whether they are big or little we trim them off one
at a time.

This seems to be the situation in the book of James. A sentence
here, a sentence there, a verse here, a verse there, yet each one
important in itself as it snips or cuts off something. Sometimes
something is added as if it were grafted in and is important.
Thus the book is like a manual of instruction for a gardener.
It would therefore be especially helpful to someone who is promoting the development and the growing of spiritual life and
spiritual experience.

The words of the fourth verse: "Let patience have her perfect work, that ye may be perfect and entire, wanting nothing,"
follow directly after the thought in verses two and three, "Count
it all joy when you fall into divers temptations; knowing this,
that the trying of your faith worketh patience. . . . " This would
seem to say in regard to the believer's experience with the Lord

that he must follow along all the way through to the finish. The important word is "patience."

How many projects have been begun but become a total loss because they have never been finished! No doubt many a woman will be reminded of making a dress. She will smile as she remembers a half finished dress tucked away in a dresser drawer. Maybe it is almost finished — but it is not complete, not really finished. She can not wear it. All the time spent on it so far does not help at all. It takes that last trimming, that last stitching, that last fitting, to make the dress what it was meant to be.

The same holds true in the raising of a crop or a garden. When the farmer wants to raise a crop he must prepare the soil at the proper time of the year. He must plant the seed in the right way. Next, he must cultivate it. He will then hoe and trim and spray his growing plants. He will try to keep the neighbor's dogs away, so that his garden and his flowers will have a chance to grow. This is how it goes with gardening.

The farmer's complete attention must be given to it in whatever way it is needed. He watches over his garden and protects it all summer long. Why does he protect his crops all summer long? The answer is easy — because he wants the harvest that he has worked and watched for.

Harvest time is the best time. It is the time the farmer looks forward to when he is planning to raise a crop. It's the finish that counts. How farmers watch their grain grow all summer waiting for harvest time. When the grain turns yellow they feel at last the time has come. They eagerly hope they will have a great harvest, because this was their purpose in all that they did.

Seeing things through to a finish is always important. Many of us who have played baseball know that unless the runner gets to home plate his hit does not count. It will not pay off to get to first base, no matter how many players get there. And it is of no particular importance to have many players reach second base; nor does it matter how many get to third base. We only score when we get to home plate. This is the way it is when we play baseball.

In football it is a matter of getting the ball over the goal line. A team may carry the ball and move it for various distances on the field, but unless they get it over the goal line they do not score. It's that last run, that last inch that really counts.

This is true in spiritual things. This is what James means when he writes, "Let patience have her perfect work." In this case the meaning of "patience" is to keep on keeping on. It is perseverance. It is persistence. It is stick-to-it-ness. If we start out doing what God wanted us to do, we keep it up to please Him. Naturally this does not mean that we will be rigid, that we will never change. It does not mean that we would not review our work. But it does mean that we will never change our purpose. We intend to be well pleasing in His sight. We start out that way. We may have been following through that way and now we are running into trouble. James says, "Keep on going through to the end."

You wanted to worship God? You wanted to serve God? Then keep right on. Continue all the way through spring time, summer time, growing time and harvest time. Watch over your field until the harvest. Stay with it all the way through. Let patience have her perfect work — "her complete operation." When you follow a certain policy with reference to your business, one that you believe is right in the sight of God, you must keep it all the way if you want to get results.

There are those who will tempt us to do wrong. If we turn them down nine times, saying "No" to them nine times — and then give in to them the tenth time, all is lost. Our testimony is no longer worth anything as far as they are concerned, for we gave in at a certain point, at a certain time. So "Let patience have her complete work," and keep on saying "No"!

James writes on to say "that you may be perfect." The word "perfect" in this instance doesn't mean "without a flaw"; "without any blemish." Rather, the meaning here is in the sense of "mature, full grown" — "fruitbearing." James is saying that you may be full grown and bearing fruit. The figure is that of a fruit tree now developed in growth to where it bears fruit. James is actually considering here that the one big project that we are to keep in mind is that we may grow into the fullness and into the stature of Christ, bearing fruit to the glory of God.

When a person becomes a believer, the one basic thing that he wants is to grow to the place where he will be walking with the Lord Jesus Christ, and will be mature in Him. This is the goal toward which all Christians are moving.

James is writing to believers that they should count it all joy when they fall into divers testings because that is the road toward maturity. It is as though a person were going to school, working to get his diploma. This means he will have to pass all courses successfully. He may make mistakes while writing an English composition. He may make mistakes in his mathematical assignment. It is possible that in the course of his studies he may have failed certain tests so that in some subjects his grades are low. But all of this is incidental to "finishing" the course and coming out as a graduate.

"That you may be perfect and entire," (finished to the final touch, all the way through) "wanting nothing." "Wanting nothing" is an old English way of saying, "lacking nothing." The Twenty-third Psalm says, "The Lord is my shepherd, I shall not want." This does not mean that the believer will never desire anything. It means that he will never *lack* anything. He will never be without anything he needs, because the Lord takes care of him.

In other words, if the believer follows this guidance he will be patient in all his experiences. He will keep on keeping on; he will not falter. He will follow on through past second base and third base to home plate. The woman with the unfinished dress will follow on through, until the dress is finished. She will keep on working on it. She may run into problems and grow tired of sewing but if she keeps on working until it is finished she will have the dress. It is the same with any experience the Christian is having. When he faces some particular problem, he must keep on with it until it is finished.

It will not do to be a Christian part of the time if the believer desires to grow and mature in Christ. It will not be good enough to live the Christian life only when things are going his way. He must stick with it all day, under all circumstances. It is true that this will bring certain trials and testings. But when he keeps on keeping on, going all the way through, he will find that the purpose of his whole Christian experience is his growth and development and maturity in spiritual things. He will be more kind, more gentle, more meek and more long suffering.

So far as living in Christ is concerned, neither trouble nor any kind of testing should frighten or scare off the believer. This is the lesson James emphasizes at the very outset, the very beginning of his letter. The believer in Christ is to keep right on trusting the Lord, so that he may grow in grace and knowledge. In the course of persevering in his obedience the Christian will develop into the kind of person that the Lord Jesus wants him to be.

Chapter 4

ASKING FOR WISDOM

> If any of you lack wisdom, let him ask of God, that giveth
> to all men liberally and upbraideth not; and it shall be given
> to him (James 1:5).

"Wisdom" means mainly, "good common sense." It is something much more significant than cleverness, or being smart in a sophisticated sense. Clever men are not always wise, or, to put it in another way, a man may be clever and yet not have "common sense." Every community has seen some smart, clever persons who have literally made fools of themselves. Sometimes such are found among our own kin, and they may be seen on any university campus. When James promises "wisdom" from God, we may be sure this means much more than being sharp or shrewd.

When I was a student at the university, there were some brilliant men on the campus. We used to say about some of these men that they did not have sense enough to come in when it rained, and often that really seemed to be the way it was.

I grew up in Canada, in the country, many years ago. We did not meet many educated people there. In our community it was a rare thing to find a man who had gone to college, but we had met some and had heard many things about them. All that we country folks remembered was that educated people could do some of the most ignorant things. I myself have been in school for many years and finally came to have my own degrees. And now I must say that the more I have come into it, the more I realize that education in itself, sophistication in itself, does not necessarily mean that a person has good sense.

This may be seen in different ways. All of us know some people with great education and clever ability, who cannot get along with each other. They cannot get along in the home or even with their neighbors. Being educated did not help them.

Every once in a while we come across a person who has inherited a great deal of money; he has become wealthy, yet he leads an utterly useless life. Some famous people whose names are known far and wide may be envied by many. But when we come to find out about them personally, we pity them. We feel sorry for them. They do not know what it is to live with themselves, let alone with anyone else.

How wonderful it is when a person has good common sense! This is particularly true around a church, where we come into Christian things, among the things that have to do with spiritual life. In the matter of Bible study, we meet people who are experts in the Bible, who teach the Bible. Yet even they can come out with the strangest ideas that they claim to get out of the Bible. Such men really give the Bible a bad name. Once in a while some such person will send me some letters through the mail that are really and truly astonishing.

We can almost tell by a man's ordinary way of life whether he has good common sense. A man with good sense will keep his yard in order. His house will be in order, and we may expect that his affairs are in order too. A man with good sense will have some idea as to how much money he owes. He will have some idea of how he will pay his debts — things like that.

If someone were to go and buy and buy, without any idea of how he could pay for it, we would say that such a person does not have good common sense. Concerning a man's common sense, he must have the ability to make comparisons and to distinguish between the big things and the little things. He must be able to evaluate things, to see the difference between something that is important and something that is unimportant.

When we come to spiritual things, things of the Bible, we find the same truth present. How wonderful it is when a person has good common sense. When he can see clearly, understand plainly, judge calmly and decide honestly. That's marvelous to see and wonderful to share.

Generally speaking we are inclined to be pessimistic about

someone who acts foolishly. As we study the Bible we are sad about anyone who is foolish, because there is really little hope in the promises of God for a fool.

Now suppose such a foolish person realizes his need and wants good sense. For him, what we read in James, is good news. "If any of you lack wisdom, let him ask of God, who giveth to all men liberally, and upbraideth not; and it shall be given him." So if a person wants good sense, what should he do? He should pray and ask of God, "who giveth." Anything we ever get from God that is really precious and worthwhile is a gift. We cannot pay for it. We cannot earn it. "He giveth to all men," means to anyone. That is the meaning of "all men." To any of us He gives liberally — without cost.

"Upbraideth not" is an old English expression which we do not use ordinarily. What this really means is, He does not scold. In other words, we come to God and ask Him to give us good sense because we have been acting the fool for many years. When we come to Him and say, "Oh Lord, just give me good sense," God will not scold us. He will not come to us and say, "You have played a fool all this time, go on and lie in the bed you have made."

One translator puts it this way, "God will give without making them foolish or guilty. God will do this without scolding. He knows our frame. He remembers that we are but dust. Just as a father pitieth his children so the Lord pitieth them that fear Him." So whoever we may be, especially if we are Christians, we may come to God. We may tell Him that we just wish that we had good sense. He will give it to all who ask. We need no particular qualifications, no payment. We only need to receive this gift. It is waiting for us, as soon as we ask, because God has already spoken.

He has already put His wisdom within my reach. I find it in the Scriptures, in the Bible, in the Word of God. So if I want wisdom I must read the Bible. I must study the Bible and get to know it. My heart and mind must be open to let the truth come in. Out of the Bible will come wisdom. That is the place where it is found. When I get on my knees and say, "Oh Lord, give me good sense," I have made a good start. I need not ask, "How will He answer my prayers? What will God do?" He will show me in His Word. He will show me in the Bible. There I will find the answer as I read and study.

Good common sense can actually be found in the Bible. God will help as I get to know Him. He will lead me in His way and He will bless me. One of the finest things that can happen to me as I turn to God is that I give up on myself. I learn to deny myself and yield to God. Just as surely as I do this, as surely as I deny myself and yield to Him, it is then that God can show me what He wants me to be. He shows it to me in the Bible.

A business man who has to face a big decision wants help. He can ask the Lord to overrule in his affairs. He can ask for guidance and God will lead and direct him, when the time comes to act. This man may not know all the reasons why this is true, but he can get wisdom by studying the Bible. Unless I read and study the Bible I am not really asking. When I read and study and pray I will come to know the mind of God. Knowing the mind of God will give me good sense and I will be most favored.

Chapter 5

LOSS IN WAVERING

> But let him ask in faith, nothing wavering. For he that wavereth is like a wave of the sea driven with the wind and tossed. For let not that man think that he shall receive any thing of the Lord. A double-minded man is unstable in all his ways (James 1:6-8).

As we read these words slowly, letting them speak to us, our attention is drawn to the fact that here James deals with specific and practical problems. He deals with each one of them singly and he makes a sharp, blunt comment about each problem he raises.

We noted previously in verse five, James writes about the matter of asking God for help and wisdom. He tells us of God's promise that when we ask for wisdom, He will give liberally, without scolding us. He will give freely to all who ask. It would appear that asking God for anything, with reservations in our hearts, is really not asking at all.

James points out, "Let him ask in faith, nothing wavering." When we ask, believing in God, we are confident that He is able to give us the wisdom we ask for. To have this faith, we really need to go to the Word of God. "Faith cometh by hearing, and hearing, by the word of God . . . " (Romans 10:17). If we do not read the Bible, nor study it, as we come to ask God for help, we are either naïve and superficial or we are just plain ignorant. Asking in faith means that we ask according to what the Scriptures teach us (Romans 10:17).

When the word, "faith," is used here, we are not referring to some will power on our part. There is no way in which we ourselves can make any promise of God come to pass. That would be what we might call, make believe. Faith depends on finding out what the promises of God are. We must seek the mind of God in His Word, and then we must receive it. We must actually commit ourselves to Him in our lives, so that we may live in His will. Asking in faith means that we are asking God for the things He has promised in His Word. In this way we ask with a hundred per cent dependence on God, nothing wavering.

Now the word, "wavering" means: one time "yes" and one time "no." First we are for it and then we are not for it. To-day we ask and tomorrow we do not ask. We begin to wonder what it would be like to be completely dependent on God, and we become fearful. We do not know if we can take it. We ask today and then fear that God will give it to us. We feel that we know the will of God, when all the time we are not sure that we want to know it. All of this is known to God. He looks into our hearts and sees our reservations. He knows when we are not prepared to commit ourselves to Him. Asking anything from God in this way is really not asking at all, for this is not asking in faith.

At such times joint prayer can be helpful. It is a very helpful thing to share our problems with someone else. When we join our hearts in prayer, when we speak out with our voices as we pray, we are more likely to be definite and exact in what we really want to say. We have God's promise that where two or three are gathered together in His Name He is present. He will do for us, when we have asked in the integrity of our heart, nothing wavering, without reservations or second thoughts, one hundred per cent committed.

Such complete faith requires that we know what is in the Word of God. Many of the things written in the Bible, especially in the epistles, are meant for us as believers, that we may know God's promises and depend on them. When we know what God has promised in Christ Jesus, we can live confidently. James writes, "For he that wavereth is like a wave of the sea driven with the wind and tossed." When we waver, when we have doubts, we are like a wave of the sea. We are then without confidence and could be affected by public opinion. When we waver as we pray, we say words but do not really mean them. We say the words but we do not believe God's promises. Such a prayer, full of big words, can only fall to the ground and is nothing. It has not moved upward. It is like a wave of the sea, driven with the wind, that's all. And "tossed" means just what we expect, up and down, up and down, all day never getting anywhere.

There is something strange about the waves of the sea. Some of us may recently have been beside a lake or even the seashore. We have observed the waves as they beat against the shore. We have watched them rushing across a lake. At such times, have we wondered what it is that actually moves across the lake? Have we stopped to realize that if all the water ran across the lake, it would pile up on the other side? The answer, of course, is simple. The water is not running anywhere. There is no current back underneath. As a matter of fact, if we stop to think we know that the water stays right where it is. What the water is doing is bobbing up and down, up and down, up and down. This is the way it is with us when we waver. We can be that way in life. It is sadly true, that we can be that way in prayer.

We pray and we do, and then we wait. Then we pray again and we wait and nothing happens. When we meet for prayer and nothing happens, let us search our hearts. Are we really laying hold on God? Do we really believe the promises of God? Are we really meeting in prayer? There are wonderful promises of God in the Bible. We have marvelous promises from God, "Who giveth liberally."

It is true that whatsoever a man sows that shall he also reap. We can go out and work and pray, but we will not reap from the grace of God unless we first commit ourselves to Him. A double-minded man is unstable in all his ways. "Unstable" means unsettled, going pro and con, both in and out, both up and down. Such a man is unstable in his thinking, in his character and throughout all his ways. When we ask of God while we are unsettled and are filled with reservations we are really not asking at all.

Chapter 6

THE WEAKNESS OF THE RICH

> Let the brother of low degree rejoice in that he is exalted:
> but the rich, in that he is made low: because as the flower of
> the grass he shall pass away. For the sun is no sooner risen
> with a burning heat, but it withereth the grass, and the flower
> thereof falleth, and the grace of the fashion of it perisheth: so
> also shall the rich man fade away in his ways (James 1:9-11).

The book of James is a letter, an epistle, that was written to
Christians about living in blessing. There are many aspects of
the truth in Christian living. There is the evangelistic aspect,
which points out to people who are not Christians why they
should become Christians. Another aspect of the truth, for instance, would be explaining to Christians how God operates,
how He plans to work in them. But James is particularly interested in discussing how Christians themselves could prosper
in what they do, and how they could do their best.

In this book we are again reminded that living the Christian
life is much like having a garden. We need the soil and the seed.
We need it well watered and well lighted, and the proper temperature — all this. In addition to all of this, we have a garden
in which before very long we will have to do something about
weeds. Just as sure as we have a garden, we have weeds. And
weeds need to be hoed out.

If we are going to produce a garden, the essential things,
such as the right soil, the right time and the right way of seeding,
is not enough. All this is important but our garden must have the
attention of the gardener. It needs to be cultivated. He is the

one who will destroy the weeds and prune the plants so that they may produce fruit.

In all that James writes, he is like a gardener. He is writing to Christians by way of helping them to get the greatest possible blessing out of living in the Lord. In his book there is no argument about turning to the Lord. It is assumed that believers who read his epistle are walking with Jesus.

What James wrote could easily be misunderstood, if we held that James wrote his letter to all men everywhere. James wrote to those who are trusting the Lord Jesus Christ for the salvation of their souls. Believers understand that Christ Jesus died for them. They are reconciled to God by the blood of the Lord Jesus Christ because they believe in Him. They belong to God. God is their Father, and He watches over them.

As believers live, as they move along in their Christian lives, it becomes obvious they must grow both in grace and in knowledge. They can have a better understanding of God's will. They can grow to a greater faith in Him, covering a wider range of aspects of their lives, and a deeper commitment to Him. All this is possible. This is the consequence of maturing in their spiritual lives.

James has written this book on nurture. He tells how to nurture spiritual life as a Christian that the believer may prosper and be blessed. Much of the course of living as it ordinarily happens depends greatly on circumstances over which the believer has very little control. Yet in this situation he can grow.

If we come to a situation where we encounter mountains, then we have the experience of climbing mountains. We certainly could never climb mountains if the mountains were not there. The same thing is true if we come to a swimming pool, or where there is a place to swim. Here we could swim. But if we were somewhere in the world where there is no water we obviously could not swim. These examples may appear simple and trite, but actually they express a profound fact: the Christian will find that he will be led by Christ in whatever place he happens to be. That is where his life is going to be lived. This is the thing to keep in mind. Christians will find guidance from God as to how to live where they are.

Some people are in circumstances which are downright poor.

Other people are in circumstances that are rich, which could be called fortunate, because they include much good fortune. Many times the poor person has nothing to do with being poor. And many times a rich person does not have a thing to do with being rich. It is common to give a rich person credit for being rich; just as it is common to blame the poor person for being poor. Such ideas are wrong in both cases. Many a person with money has it because the wealth was poured on him quite apart from anything he personally did.

A young minister, when he had been converted to the Lord Jesus Christ, wanted to win others to the Lord. Preaching in a certain place, he was most unhappy because he was not receiving new converts into the church. Burdened because the year's work showed that few people had come to the Lord, he came to counsel with me about his situation. Upon talking and checking with him it appeared that most of the people had been living there for years and were not about to change. It was that kind of a situation.

I suggested to this young minister that it would be an easy thing for a man who went fishing and who was really hoping to catch fish, to become downright discouraged if he caught nothing. However, it could be a good idea to find out if there were any fish to catch in that lake. I told him plainly, "If there are no fish in the lake, you can't catch any." This talk helped that young minister a great deal. He later moved to another community where there were fish, and was soon catching them.

Now let us see what James has to say in Chapter 1, verses 9-11. In these three verses James contrasts the poor and the rich. We should always realize that when we call a person poor, we are using a relative term. Poor in one country is not poor in another. Poor for one person is not poor for another person. It is the same with the rich. Rich is not an absolute specific term. We are rich only under certain conditions in comparison with others.

A brother of low degree may, in fact, be found in various situations. He may be in low degree so far as his family is concerned. He may be in low degree so far as his country is concerned. A brother of low degree may be of low degree compared to other people. He may not be well off. On the other hand, the same is true of the rich. You can find those who are rich in family because they were born into it. They may be rich in money because it was given to them. They are rich in their country because they have been born in that particular country. But the experience of each, in whatever context, is very similar.

A person who is poor, in poor circumstances, feels downright unfortunate. A person who is rich and in fortunate circumstances is inclined to feel prosperous, satisfied, and full of himself. Christians, however, should carefully consider their own state. Those who feel poor can rejoice because they have a better prospect ahead of them. They will not always be poor. On the other hand those who feel rich might keep in mind that it may not always be that way.

There is a story told of a general who sat at dinner at the royal court, seated beside the court chaplain. This commanding general turned to the minister and wanting to make conversation, inquired, "Pastor, in this moment that we are together here, could you tell me something about heaven?" The court chaplain looked at him carefully and said, "Well, yes I could. The first thing I would tell you, general, is that in heaven you will not be a general." This is something that anyone who is rich and fortunate should keep in mind.

A rich person may be easily deceived. He may be deceived into a feeling that he does not need anything. Because of this it could actually be of the goodness of God that this rich person should experience reverses. The "rich" feeling can mislead the heart into a false security. To have trouble can actually be helpful. This is true not only with money but it is also true in other ways.

For a person who is rich in home and family, living in a wonderful home and coming from a wonderful family, it is hard to see life on the other side of the tracks. The fortunate person is apt to become selfish and callous, perhaps even proud. Sometimes, under the providence of God it takes something like death, something like the loss of friends, to bring him to the realization that even his loved ones could be taken from him. The same is true with money. People who are rich, who have much money, can become thoughtless of others to the point that is actually sinful.

Sometimes rich people learn that riches have wings. Money

may easily be lost. Even this may prove to be a fortunate thing. James tells us that a Christian can prosper in adversity. This principle will operate in every case, and an intelligent Christian will be guided according to all of this. When we are poor we rejoice and are glad when good fortune comes to us. When we are rich, we should be wise enough to keep the distressing realities of life before us that we might be kept humble, because in this the health and welfare of our eternal soul is involved.

Chapter 7

BLESSING IN ENDURANCE

Blessed is the man that endureth temptation: for when he is
tried, he shall receive the crown of life, which the Lord hath
promised to them that love him (James 1:12).

James in his writing wants to make sure that believers will not
miss the blessing which God has for them. He wants them to
realize, if at all possible, that the blessing which comes out of
trouble will appear afterwards — after their troubles are over and
past.

The Lord Jesus had said so clearly: "I am come that they
might have life, and that they might have it more abundantly . . ." (John 10:10). James has in mind that God wants His
people, those who believe in Him, to have life with all His
blessings. This is why he writes so confidently of the blessing
which the patient man will receive.

When our own potential, whatever we could possibly be or do,
is realized, when our own interest is love toward God and man,
we have an abundant "life." When we know the peace of God
which passes all understanding, then we have "life" abundantly.
Now this is what the Lord has promised to all who belong to
Him: that they might have abundant life. This life comes basically, originally, out of the spiritual, in the spiritual. That is to say
it comes to a man through his spirit. It comes from God and it
has to do with the presence of God.

In other words it is not a matter of silver and gold. There is
a minimum amount of material goods which we need to satisfy
our hunger and our thirst. We need money for our needs; but
money alone will not give us "abundant life." There are rich

people whose hearts are dead. They have everything to satisfy their elemental needs. They may feel perfectly satisfied with what they have, since they cannot think of a single thing they need that they don't have, but this does not necessarily make them happy. Some extremely rich persons who have everything their hearts can desire are most unhappy people.

The specific blessings, which together make possible abundant life, come in the spiritual realm from God through the Lord Jesus Christ. Commonly we speak of this life which comes from God as eternal life. The "natural" man cannot receive this. A person who is thinking naturally is not able to understand what we are talking about. To him it is foolishness.

But the natural man has a real problem. He is inclined to think that the way in which he will get what will make life full and satisfactory is to go out and work for it. And he will try this very procedure to get it. He'll scratch around and gather around and seek to bring together enough to satisfy his needs, enough to do for him. He will try in every possible way to achieve that goal; but his goal will ever become larger and larger: he cannot attain it. That is the way a natural man thinks about living. But that is not the Gospel.

The spiritual man knows that God will give him everything he needs. God will take care of him, and God will watch over him. He can rest himself in God. Because man is first born in the natural realm, the natural gets a big start in the man. The spiritual comes later and therefore ordinarily is weaker. Even after a man becomes a Christian, he has a natural human nature because he was born naturally. When he has been born again spiritually there is in him also a life from God.

Now what creates the problem is that a Christian has in him these two principles, these two natures. He has in him both the flesh and the Spirit, and because these two are contrary one to the other he feels an inner sense of frustration. He cannot do the evil he wants to do, because the Spirit won't let him. He cannot do all the good he wants to do, because the flesh won't let him. And so being in a position betwixt and between, he has a sense of unhappiness.

However, there is hope in him because he does have the Spirit in him. God helps him out. It is a good deal like the garden we have referred to before. We have our beans out there, and we have the weeds growing too. What we do then is to hoe out the weeds to give the beans a chance to grow. The same thing is true spiritually. We have in us the Spirit of God through the Gospel. We also have in us the flesh, which is the result of being a human being. They are both in us: both the Spirit and the flesh. And so, as surely as this is the way, something must be done. The flesh must be denied, that the Spirit might grow.

Trouble helps to create situations in which we can deny the flesh. Trouble will come at us in such a way that as we face it as Christians the flesh is denied and is crucified. This is what James had in mind when he said, "Blessed is the man that endureth temptation (testing): for when he is tried, he shall receive the crown of life . . . " (James 1:12). What James calls "temptation" we could call "trouble." It has to do with testing. In the kind of temptation James is talking about, when we are put to the test we have tension and we have trouble. God's will in our spirit is to do one thing and the desire in the flesh is to do differently.

James tells us that when we endure, when we live through temptation, we will be blessed. Blessed is the man that endureth, that goes all the way through temptation, through the situation that is facing him. The only way he can get through with it, however, is by denying the flesh. Blessed is the man, who has not only experienced temptation, but who has completed the test. To be put to the test and to be tried, to reach completion, means denial of self.

When we have endured to the end, then we shall receive "the crown of life." The "crown of life" is not something we produce by our own efforts. Yet it is our efforts and our experiences that will be crowned with a victor's crown. In ancient times a wreath was put on the brow of a man who won the race. The prize, the wreath which God gives to us, is life. This will actually be given to us for God has promised this to them that love Him.

In the course of this experience of testing we are guided by the principle of God's love for us, and our love for Him. Every issue we face would then involve our decision whether to follow the desires of the flesh or follow the leading of the Spirit. It would involve our choice, whether we would do what Christ wants us to do, or what our old nature wants us to do. The principle that guides and strengthens us to do what Christ wants us to do is our love of God.

"We love him, because he first loved us" (I John 4:19). So in response to the love of God we will obey His Word. He has said, "He that loveth me, keepeth my commandments" (John 14: 21, paraphrased). In any given situation, we who love Him will obey His Word for that situation. James does not press this point. We who are Christians should keep in mind that the disposition to obey God when "self" is involved, comes from above. This is something put into our hearts by the Holy Spirit of God. No human being is good enough to do this of himself.

Christ came to give life "to them that love Him." In no other way could we come through and be victorious. The origin of the disposition to obey God, in any Christian is, "Christ in you, the hope of glory" (Colossians 1:27). When the Holy Spirit activates the will of Christ in us, it will be to obey Almighty God. We will receive the inward strength coming from God by the grace of God to obey and love Him in a troubled situation. An inward strength will bring us through to the victor's crown which is the fullness of life eternal. This is why it is a blessed thing to endure every trial and every testing.

Chapter 8

DESIRE CAUSES TEMPTATION

> Let no man say when he is tempted, I am tempted of God: for God cannot be tempted with evil, neither tempteth he any man: but every man is tempted, when he is drawn away of his own lust, and enticed. Then when lust hath conceived, it bringeth forth sin: and sin, when it is finished, bringeth forth death (James 1:13-15).

We shall be keeping in mind as we read this book that James is writing to Christians. In his first chapter which we are now studying, James begins by discussing trouble. At this point, all of us could meet him because every one of us, at one time or another, has experienced trouble. Let us all stop for a moment to consider what we actually mean by trouble. Trouble may take the form of serious, perhaps incurable illness. There may be loss of our property. There may be separation from loved ones. There may be quarreling and misunderstanding. There may be failure or defeat. There may be disappointment and distress because of unkindness and cruelty. That's trouble.

Of course we may have trouble in many other ways too. People may make trouble for us, but James writes about ordinary troubles which we all face. He points out in Chapter 1:2-4 that trouble may result in real benefit because it can cultivate patience in us. Such patience will bring experience, and experience will bring hope. All of this is really a good thing for us. When we are in trouble we will turn to God and ask for wisdom by which to be guided. James points out that sometimes trouble can actually help us by humbling us, and that is good for us. We read in verse twelve, that to benefit from trouble, we must

live it through. When we stop in the midst of it and then try
to run away from it, we will benefit not at all.

James wants to keep the record straight, by making it clear
in verses 13 - 15, that all forms of trouble and temptation originate
in the human heart. The things we actually prefer will bring
about our troubles, since we can be tempted only by what we
like. We can be troubled inwardly only because of things we
want to do, and the things we desire.

"Let no man say when he is tempted, I was tempted of God;
for God cannot be tempted with evil, · neither tempteth he any
man." In this verse James analyzes what actually happens in a
man. He starts out by saying, "Don't blame God for the kind
of temptation, the particular kind of trouble which befalls you.
It will befall you because you are you, because of what you are
like." This analysis will not seem adequate and complete to all
of us, but surely we are all prepared to agree with James when
he says, "Do not blame God." It is true that the providence
of God permits the temptation, but God does not push us into it.
He does not force us to want a new car when we cannot afford it.
God does not make us want to spend money when we should be
saving it. God does not make us want to eat and drink what
will harm us. It is we ourselves who want to do these things.
We want that car, or want to go off on that weekend that will
cost us a lot of money. We ourselves want to do these various
things which will not be good for us. It is never God who
makes us do it. It is our wanting and liking the wrong things,
that causes trouble.

"God cannot be tempted with evil, neither tempteth he any
man." This is to say that God in Himself could never be attracted by anything that is evil. He could never use anything
that is evil to attract any man. We can just understand in our
own minds that acting in a self-willed fashion and doing as we
please is evil. Such an attitude will never come from God. God
will never orient a man to want to do as he pleases.

Some of us will wonder about the temptation of Jesus of
Nazareth in the desert when we read, "God is not tempted with
evil." As we look back to that experience of Jesus of Nazareth
being tempted by Satan in the desert, we find that He was not
tempted with evil. He was tempted about bread, and there is

nothing evil about that. He was tempted about trusting God. Nothing evil about that. He was tempted about serving God, by being ruler over kingdoms. Nothing evil about that.

The Lord Jesus could not have been tempted with the things that tempt us. In our sinful nature and condition, we could be tempted with things that are actually wrong. We can be tempted to act selfishly, immorally, sinfully. Jesus of Nazareth could never have been tempted to do anything selfishly. In His temptation in the wilderness, He was tempted to do things which in themselves were quite proper. He would not do them because they were not in the will of His Father.

Evil, then, is acting in self-will, doing what we want to do when we want to do it. Nothing like that will ever come from God. That would come right out of our own hearts. In verse 14 we read, "Every man is tempted [he is put to the test] when he is drawn away of his own lust [his inward desire]. . . . " Now our inward desires are sinful because we are sinful. We do not have to be that way. In the case of our Lord Jesus Christ, no inward desires as He had them could have been sinful. His inward desire at all times was to please His Father. Through all His being, from the bottom of His heart, Christ wanted to do those things which were pleasing in the sight of God. This is righteousness and goodness.

We, on the other hand, want to do the things that please us. Now we may not always feel this desire to please ourselves so vividly. Still, when all is said and done, at the time we are tempted into things that are not right and good, it is because of something we personally want. When James goes on to say, "when lust hath conceived," he refers to the kind of conceiving in which an idea or a plan is produced by our own desires. For instance we might say: "Do you have any conception of what you will do Saturday afternoon? or what conception do you have of next Friday night? What idea do you have about it? Do you have a conception of what we will do at the picnic?" "When lust hath conceived," when ideas are formed and developed, there follows action. Sin comes when we act and do.

Now we should keep in mind that being tempted, being confronted with the inward desire to action, is not in itself necessarily sin. Such desires may be sinful, and inclined to sin, but just having the inclination is not necessarily sin, even though it maybe sinful. We act to please ourselves, when we have in mind to do what we want to do, when we want to do it. When we get sinful ideas and the ideas grow and we finally do it, that's sin. The doing is sin.

"Then when lust hath conceived, it bringeth forth sin: and sin, when it is finished, bringeth forth death." When we finally act in self service, doing something to satisfy ourselves, this brings forth death. That is to say, it induces a state in us that the Bible calls death. Such a state is a separation from God. The moment we went in our own way we were alienated from God. We became strangers to Him.

Chapter 9

GOOD GIFTS ARE FROM GOD

Do not err, my beloved brethren. Every good gift and every
perfect gift is from above, and cometh down from the Father
of lights, with whom is no variableness, neither shadow of
turning. Of his own will begat he us with the word of truth,
that we should be a kind of first fruits of his creatures (James
1:16-18).

These words hold a vital message for all Christians. It is
meant for those who have received the Lord Jesus Christ as
Saviour and who have been forgiven. These have been received
into the family of God and adopted as the children of God.

God has regenerated believers and put His Holy Spirit in
them. Now the Holy Spirit in the Christian moves him to do
the will of God.

As Christians we continue to have in our bodies our old human
natures, the flesh, with all that is involved in the flesh. But in
every believer who lives as a Christian in this world there is also
the new man which is in him by the grace of God. The old
nature in us wants us to take credit to ourselves. How natural
it is for any man to take credit for anything good that he has
done. When we are in action, and what we are doing turns out
well, we want people to appreciate the fact that we did it.
Smilingly we accept all the praise and the congratulations and
consider it as our just due. If it should turn out that the thing
we did was bad, we do not want to be told about it. We'd
rather blame our mistakes on someone else. This is as natural
as it is human.

The new man in any Christian knows that if there is anything
good in his actions and doings the glory belongs to God. As

Christians we do not take credit to ourselves but give all praise and glory to our Lord Jesus Christ.

James 1:16 gives an important warning: "Do not err, my beloved brethren." Don't make any mistakes. James then tells the exact truth, the real truth. "Every good gift and every perfect gift is from above, and cometh down from the Father of lights, with whom is no variableness, neither shadow of turning." In these words two basic virtues in the ways of God are implied: God is generous, giving liberally; God is faithful and honest in His attitude. He alone is consistent and reliable. These are the two virtues that constitute godliness. When inside our own hearts there is honesty, consistency and reliability; when in our actions with people we are gracious and generous and charitable; then we have godliness.

In contrast, sin is self-centered. Sin promotes the opposite of a life which is interested in others, and helpful toward others. The orientation of any natural person is inward. When we have this sinful consciousness in our hearts we think only of ourselves. Because we are interested in ourselves, we guard ourselves. We have to make something of ourselves. If there is anything around us, we grab for ourselves. If there is anything within reach, we take it. Whatever we get, we keep. This is the way with our natural self. This is the opposite of love and is the essence of ungodliness.

When we are oriented first to God we have love in our hearts. We think about the love of God who sent His Son to die for us: "God commended his love toward us, in that, while we were yet sinners, Christ died for us (Romans 5:8). So far as we, who are Christians, are concerned in our spiritual life, our first consciousness is toward God. From out of this grows a sense of appreciation for the creation which God has made, which includes all men. So that with reference to other people, we now want to give and to share. This may sound fanciful to some, but to a Christian there is nothing fanciful about this. This is the truth; this is real. When we are born again and the Spirit of God is within us, our sinful self-centered natural self is submerged.

Christians are oriented in two ways: first, upward to God, and then outward to God's creation; first to God, then toward man.

They now are inclined toward God, wanting to please Him, and toward man, wanting to help him. Christians have the disposition to take of their own, and share it with other men, giving to any man.

The Lord Jesus said, "If any man will come after me, let him deny himself, and take up his cross, and follow me" (Matthew 16:24). The center of all our trouble is self. Interest in self causes our problems and love of self causes our sinfulness. James has pointed out every man is tempted when he is drawn away by his own lust, by his inward desires, by himself. When this lust, his own personal desire for himself, has conceived, it bringeth forth death.

When a soul thinks about God and others, this is godly; this is different. Now there is something going on, moving toward God. Now every giving is good. That is the meaning of this "good gift." It does not make a comparison — one gift over against another. Every gift which the Christian is giving to people, giving to others, is good.

A gift becomes "perfect" when it is a completed gift: as when we mean to do people good and then actually carry it out.

"Every good gift and every perfect gift is from above, and cometh down from the Father of lights, with whom is no variableness." These words, "Father of lights," are a reference to the book of Genesis. When God created the heavens and the earth, He said, "Let there be light: and there was light" (Genesis 1:3). Afterwards He said, "Let there be light bearers and He created the sun, moon and stars" (paraphrase). In this way God, the Creator is considered the Father of lights. Light is something the world could not do without. Neither plants nor anything else could grow without light. Scientists tell us that light is a necessary form of energy. God gives light. He gives us what it takes to live by. This discussion conveys the idea that light is a gift from God. With God there "is no variableness, neither shadow of turning." He does not change. He is always constant. This supply of light and energy so essential to life will never be cut off.

James then goes on to say, "Of his own will begat he us with the word of truth, that we should be a kind of first fruits of his creatures." This does not speak of human nature as such. It does not refer to mankind. This refers to Christians. "Of his own will begat he us, with the word of truth." This is not how mankind was originated. God begets believers by the word of truth. In other words, the whole plan of salvation is His. The Gospel is His own perfect gift to man.

Man is just naturally full of what he can do, and he takes all the credit to himself. In our day and time the whole world has been astonished, and has been frightened, by the "bomb." Man put the bomb together, man made the bombs go off, but the power was not supplied by man. God created all power; but natural man does not credit God with this.

Gardens are so beautiful that people often go for miles to admire some particularly beautiful garden. In such a garden grow lovely fragrant flowers. Not a single blossom would be there if God had not made them grow, yet natural man does not credit God with this.

In referring to all the wonders of science, we might well ask, who made the scientists? In science man manipulates the universe and uses energy which God has provided. Man only manipulates and moves around the elements which God has made.

Even so He begat us with the word of truth, with the Gospel. The Gospel is the seed "that we should be a kind of first fruits" (James 1:18). Born again, regenerated Christians are to be first fruits, samples for the whole world to see: what God can do and will do in His work of salvation.

Chapter 10

HEAR WITH MEEKNESS

Wherefore, my beloved brethren, let every man be swift to hear, slow to speak, slow to wrath: for the wrath of man worketh not the righteousness of God. Wherefore lay apart all filthiness and superfluity of naughtiness, and receive with meekness the engrafted word, which is able to save your souls (James 1:19-21).

There is a very real reason why we as Christians should live in obedience to God. These words of admonition tell us something important. They tell us that God does not ask us to be good because we are able to be good. The truth of the matter is that we cannot be good. God also does not expect us to be good to get something out of it. It does not follow that because we are good we are going to be rich. God wants us to be, and to do good. He wants us to demonstrate to the whole world how differently we live, when we no longer walk alone in our strength and depend on our own understanding, but rather walk with our hand in His. In this we show forth the righteousness which comes from God.

God sent His Son Jesus Christ into the world to seek and to save the lost. Now God wants to show all mankind how we, who have been saved, look and act as we walk with Him. In this way all can see what it means to be saved. When we accepted Christ as our Saviour, the first idea that came to us was that He would save us from the penalty of our sins. We remember to this day our real sense of relief and satisfaction, and the thanksgiving in our hearts, just to know that He had saved us from hell and destruction. To this moment we rejoice in the assurance that Christ died for us, and gave Himself to us. We were guilty, we had done wrong, and we were debtors before God; but in His grace He secured our forgiveness and reconciled us to God.

Since we have been redeemed, we can be delivered now from the sinful ways to which we were committed. We can be delivered, truly and completely delivered, from our bad habits. It may well be true there are Christians who are not fully delivered, but they could be delivered. It could be that some would say: "I am on the road; I am on the way; but I am not altogether delivered." This is possible because it is undoubtedly true that any one of us can shorten or curtail or cut down the complete effectiveness of God's promise to us. But God has promised to set us free and He will do it if we let Him.

We can be delivered and regenerated in and by the grace of God through the Lord Jesus Christ. With His Holy Spirit in us, we can have fellowship in our union with Him. All this comes to our minds and is our first line of thought when we receive Christ Jesus into our hearts and lives. It is enough to make us joyful and happy and glad and thankful to God, who has given all this to us.

Then something else follows. Sooner or later it will come for sure. "We love him, because he first loved us" (I John 4:19). When it dawns on us how much God has done for us, it affects us inside so that we love Him. In love we want to please Him. It becomes our joy to give Him pleasure. It is the love of God who loved us that is the real dynamic in Christian living. "Herein is love, not that we loved God, but that he loved us, and sent his Son to be the propitiation for our sins" (I John 4:10).

So actually when we obey God, when we walk with God, and when we serve God, we do this not because we have to: we do this because we want to.

In James 1:19 - 21 James addresses himself to willing people. He is talking to loving people. He writes to people that want to be well pleasing in the sight of God. When love is operating, even human love between people, the person who loves another person wants to do for that person. When we are in love, we want to please our loved ones. This is a natural feeling we have. It is a real dynamic. It causes us to do things because we love. We want to see the faces of our loved ones light up with joy.

We want to help them just to see them smile. This is the very thing James is talking about.

James goes on to say: "Wherefore, my beloved brethren." He uses the word love, calling them "beloved." He has in mind they have been loved of God, and therefore they are loving Him. Then he says: "Let every man be swift to hear, slow to speak, slow to wrath." In all this James is implying every beloved Christian, every beloved brother, who is loving God, will be "swift to hear, slow to speak, slow to wrath, for the wrath of man, worketh not the righteousness of God." And since this is the case James urges to "lay apart all filthiness and superfluity of naughtiness, and receive with meekness the engrafted word, which is able to save your souls."

These words spoken to loving willing people are very important even if they sound unusual to us. When we talk to others, we seldom use the word "filthy" in this sense. We do not speak of "laying apart all filthiness." There are various ways in which we could express this. It would be the same thing if one of us should say: "Quit your meanness." It would read and sound differently and it would not be as close to the original Greek text, but the same meaning would be there. One of the most recent versions of the New Testament expresses this passage thus: "Have done, then, with impurity and every other evil which touches the lives of others, and humbly accept the message that God has sown in your hearts, and which can save your souls" (James 1:21, Phillips).

In verse 19 we read, "Let every man be swift to hear." The opposite of that would be simply "slow to listen." The Christian should not be like that. Again we read: "Slow to speak." The opposite of that would simply be "hasty words." James writes on: "Slow to wrath." The opposite of that would be "quick to take offense." Putting all these together: "being slow to listen to God," using "hasty words in argument," and being "quick to take offense," all this would be sin, all the way up and down; just plain sin. James says to us as Christians, "Do not be like that, because then you will never promote righteousness." When we want to promote righteousness we must be swift to hear God. We must be slow to speak when our turn comes, and be slow to wrath.

These wonderful words of admonition in verse 21 have been variously translated. One recent version, the *New English Bible* presents this translation: "Each one of you must be quick to listen, slow to speak, and slow to be angry. (Verse 19) For a man's anger cannot promote the justice of God. (Now verse 21) Away then with all that is sordid, and the malice that hurries to excess, and quietly accept the message planted in your hearts, which can bring you salvation." Another translation *(Today's English Version)* reads as follows: "Rid yourselves, then of every filthy habit and all wicked conduct. Submit to God and accept the word that he plants in your hearts, which is able to save you." Still another translation shows us how the same thing can be said in still another way. "So get rid of all uncleanness and the rampant outgrowth of wickedness, and in a humble, (gentle, modest) spirit, receive and welcome the Word, which implanted and rooted [in your hearts] contains the power to save your soul" (James 1:21, Amplified).

These translations are not just words someone has made up. Scholars who have studied the Greek language carefully and faithfully have been able to express the same thought differently. When James writes, "lay apart all filthiness" we can be sure of one thing: anything that is selfish is dirty in a spiritual sense, and must be wiped off. "The superfluity of naughtiness" refers to evil impulses just overflowing, welling out like a spring. It is actually an old English expression meaning "ugly sin." "Receive with meekness" means: when the Word of God judges us, and we hear some very straight things said to us from the Word of God, we must receive such meekly, without anger. "The engrafted word" means that, when God's Word is preached to us, the Holy Spirit enables it to grip our hearts. It is as though His Word like a plant had been grafted into our consciousness. This Word is able to save our souls as we surrender our own wills and respond to it. We praise God for the engrafted Word through which all who believe may be saved.

Chapter 11

DOERS NOT HEARERS

But be ye doers of the word, and not hearers only, deceiving your own selves . . . be blessed in his deed (James 1:22, 25).

These words express a plain, almost blunt message that cannot be misunderstood. They present a serious aspect of the truth. It is really an old truth, which points to a common snare for any one of us. Many realize that we could actually deceive ourselves in matters of faith. We may believe on the Lord Jesus Christ. We may have accepted Him as our Saviour and committed ourselves to Him. Yet James points out to us that we may not be prospering as we should in spiritual things, growing in grace and knowledge. He puts before us a clear distinction between people who are doers and those who are hearers only. Of course, the doer has to be a hearer also. Both start out by hearing the Word. But after the Word is heard some hearers do and others don't do. Often we discuss whether to do or not to do, whether to choose or not to choose. Finally we come to a decision. We say we are going to do this — then we may go home and do nothing. This is especially true in matters of religion and in the life of faith.

How often we argue heatedly about which is the best version, the best translation of the Bible. We can really get emotionally worked up about it. The contention can be so sharp that we can actually cause trouble in families and among friends, and between people who never read the Bible anyway. What difference in the wide world does it make which version we favor, if we do not read it? The tragedy is that many of us deceive ourselves into thinking that we are believers because we argue about the Bible.

"Be ye doers of the word, and not hearers only." This does not mean that every time we go into a church and listen to a man preach, that we are hearing the Word. Suppose this preacher gets up and spends all his time telling us that what we ought to be doing is working over here, down the street, doing something in a certain area. Is that preaching the Word? Suppose a preacher were to spend all his time telling us that we ought to support a certain political candidate. Is that preaching the Word? Suppose that someone takes time to tell us that what other people in the world are doing and spends his time describing how terrible people in certain other countries are, and that we should be doing something about it: would that be preaching the Word? Would those listening to such preaching have the opportunity to hear the Word? Surely we know better than that! "Doers" refers to "doers of the Word of God," as presented in the Gospel of Jesus Christ (I Corinthians 15:1 - 5).

So far as we are concerned, the Word of God is that we should believe on the Lord Jesus Christ. It is not enough simply to know about Him, we must also believe on Him. It is very much like going to our doctor who tells us what to do. He prescribes a certain medicine which comes in capsule form and which we are to take three times a day. So, we go to the store and buy the medicine and take it home. The snare we are liable to fall into is thinking we did what the doctor prescribed because we bought the medicine, when actually we did not do it. Thinking we had taken it cannot help us. We all know that we need to take the capsule in our fingers, open our mouth and swallow it. Then we are doers, not hearers only. Buying the medicine and putting it into the medicine cabinet is only deceiving ourselves, fooling ourselves, that we are doing what the doctor told us to do. Unless we yield ourselves to obey Him, we do not really believe in Him.

In verses 23 and 24 we see the danger signals set out. These verses are by way of explanation and argument. "If any be a hearer of the word" — if he really heard what he was supposed to do, — "and not a doer" — he does not act on what he has heard: "He is like unto a man beholding his natural face in a glass: for he beholdeth himself, and goeth his way, and straightway forgetteth what manner of man he was." In other words a person could look into a mirror and see that his face is dirty. If he does not wash it, he can forget it. Sure he saw it. Sure, it was true. But if he does nothing about it, he can forget it. In the same way, there lies a danger in attending church services. Many, many times we go to church, waiting for the minister to stir us. We count him a good preacher if he can stir our feelings. But if we get all aroused listening to him, and do nothing about it, the whole church service could actually work to our hurt. There would be the danger of our becoming hardened to the call of the Gospel.

We can not excuse ourselves by saying that we do not always know what to do. Let us stop and think. Did the preacher say that we should worship God? Was he saying, for example, that we should pray? Did we feel deep down in our hearts that we should pray? When we listened to the preacher and were moved to pray because we knew that he had told us the truth, did we pray? If we did not pray we would be further back than we were before we went to church. Some referee is going to blow the whistle on us and give us a five yard penalty for delaying the game. To be moved in emotion and then to have no action — not to do anything — results in depression.

It becomes sadly obvious why and how some of us have developed a deep rooted depression about our spiritual life. Actually we should feel badly if we have not prayed, if we have not read our Bible, if we have not taken anything out of our pockets to give to missions, or talked to anyone about the Lord. Impression without expression leads to depression. I picked these words up when I was down in Brazil. I remember going through a church building one day, where all the signs and literature were in the Portuguese language, and where all the people spoke Portuguese. Suddenly I came across a blackboard on which was written a paragraph in the English language. The very first words I read were these, "Impression without expression leads to depression." I did not hear a better thing in Brazil in six weeks. This is exactly the way in which it works. The truth to be noted is clear and simple: to avoid depression, when we feel led to pray, let us pray. Let us pray not only because of what and for whom we will pray, but for our own sakes. When we go to church and feel led to give to missions, let us give. We may not have expected to give to missions when we came into the service, but let us control ourselves and dig down into our pockets or purses and hand out some money: let us give to the missions. This is the way of blessing.

"But whoso looketh into the perfect law of liberty, and continueth therein, he being not a forgetful hearer, but a doer of the work, this man shall be blessed in his deed" (James 1:25). "The perfect law of liberty" — this is the way to be free. Do we really know this way? To be truly free means: dying in the Lord, buried with Him, raised from the dead, filled with the Spirit. This law of liberty is perfect, complete, when carried through to completion: carried all the way through. "Whoso looketh into the perfect law of liberty" — whoso looketh into the truth of how to really get to be filled with the Holy Spirit of God, and continues therein, "This man will be blessed in his deed."

We think of harvest as a time of blessing. By the way, if we wanted to harvest beans we would first plant them, then cultivate and irrigate them. We would hoe out the weeds, and hill the beans during the summer. In due time we would have our harvest — our blessing. All this comes to our minds as we study the book of James and think about the whole matter of living in faith in the Lord.

Chapter 12

PURE RELIGION

> If any man among you seem to be religious, and bridleth not his tongue, but deceiveth his own heart, this man's religion is vain. Pure religion and undefiled before God and the Father is this, To visit the fatherless and widows in their affliction, and to keep himself unspotted from the world (James 1:26-27).

Could we ourselves tell anyone in so many words what real religion is? The word religion is not much used in the Bible. We seldom find it in the New Testament. We use it far more in conversation than the Bible uses it. James uses it and gives the clearest statement about religion in the whole Bible.

"If any man among you seem to be religious." What is meant by the word religious? As it is commonly used "religion" refers to our conduct and behavior in response to our concept of God. It is our personal response to Him as we consider and think about Him. Now take note of the words, "among you." This is not broad and long, over the whole world. This is among Christians. So James is saying if there is any man among believers, who sets himself up as a person who is really responding to the truth of God, claiming to be a religious person, but who does not control his talk, "bridleth not his tongue," he is deceiving his own heart. Such a man who does not control his tongue is fooling himself: "This man's religion is vain." The word "vain" means empty, meaningless. James was saying, "This man's religion doesn't mean anything of value."

There are many evidences of "vain religion." When we argue a lot, when we are not careful about our speech, we are not yielded to God. When we are unkind in what we say to other people, when we are nasty in our criticisms, we are only pretending to be yielded. Our religion is vain.

The clearest statement about pure religion in the New Testament is found in verse 27: "Pure religion and undefiled before God and the Father is this, to visit the fatherless and widows in their affliction, and to keep himself unspotted from the world." We should note the fact that James wrote "pure religion and undefiled before God and the Father." By mentioning "the Father" James brought in everything about the Christian Gospel. The words, "God the Father," are not used. anywhere else than with reference to the Lord Jesus Christ. By using these words James indicates he has the religion of a Christian in mind. The conduct he describes is a direct response to what Jesus Christ revealed in Himself about God.

"Pure religion and undefiled." Religion is pure if there is nothing selfish in it. It is undefiled if there is nothing proud about it. Our religion is undefiled when our conduct in response to God is not motivated for any personal advantage. The real genuine response to the true God is this: "to visit the fatherless and the widows in their afflictions." This includes all people who really need help in their affliction. Visiting them is to come to help them.

We are reminded of an incident in the life of our Lord Jesus Christ. When He was asked which was the greatest commandment, He answered, "Thou shalt love the Lord thy God. . . ." (Matthew 22:37). Then He went on to say, "The second is like unto it, Thou shalt love thy neighbour as thyself" (Matthew 22:39). One man willing to justify himself asked this question, "And who is my neighbour?" (Luke 10:29). Our Lord Jesus told the story of the Good Samaritan, who coming along the road, saw someone in need. Because this person was in need he went to him, and he shared what he had with the man in need. This is love in action. This is what Jesus meant by saying "love your neighbor."

"We love him, because he first loved us. Herein is love; not that we loved God, but that he loved us, and sent his Son to be the propitiation (to die) for our sins (us)" (I John 4:19, 10).

When we have been affected by the love of God, we have a genuine response to Him. We love Him because He first loved us. When we are inwardly, sincerely affected by this love of God, we will show it. We will go to the needy in their distress and help them in their need.

"And will keep himself unspotted from the world." This is a rather specific way of talking about self-denial. "Unspotted from the world." It is helpful for us, in our interpretation of the New Testament, to remember how the Apostle John writes of the "world" in his first epistle, chapter 2, verse 16. Here we read, "For all that is in the world, the lust of the flesh, and the lust of the eyes, and the pride of life . . . is of the world" (I John 2:16). This actually summarizes everything that the Bible refers to as "the flesh." This is not of God. When we become disciples of the Lord Jesus Christ we must begin by denying ourselves. ". . . let him deny himself, take up his cross, and follow me" (Matthew 16:24) are the words of our Lord. Denying ourselves means that we deny the desires of the flesh. We deny the desire of the eyes. We deny our personal pride. Everything that has to do with imagination, that has to do with vanity and pride, we now repudiate. When we can repudiate those things and keep them out of our thoughts, our conduct and our actions, we will be unspotted by the world, in our service of God. This is pure religion and undefiled: genuine, sincere, whole-hearted response to the God and Father of the Lord Jesus Christ, and to the whole truth as we find it in the Gospel.

In our day it has become a common thing to have people imply that it is only in recent years that people have become conscious of the poor. This is ridiculous. All through the history of the church, from the very first, when men were much more savage than they are today, and times were much much harder than they are today, wherever the Gospel has gone there followed kindness and help for the poor and needy. It is under the auspices of the Gospel in the strength of the message of Jesus Christ that hospitals have been built, old folks homes have been organized and orphanages have been set up. No other name in the world has ever been associated with helping the poor and the weak, the fatherless and those in distress like the name of the Lord Jesus Christ.

James 1:26 - 27 brings to our minds that it makes all the difference in the world who we think that God is, or what we think that God wants. We must never assume, that so far as God is concerned, He is someone we meet in a church building, that by simply going inside the church we are worshiping God. Walking into a church service and sitting in a pew, and staying there for an hour, is surely not worshiping God. We might be able to fool our neighbors that way, but we certainly would not fool God. When we walk into the presence of God and we sit in church for an hour or so, the actual sitting there in the church does not mean a thing. If we are thinking of a football game we saw the day before, or we think about a business deal we hope to make the next day, or a date we will go on that night, we are not worshiping God, and God knows it. Other people might not know but God looks on the heart. He knows.

If there is such a thing as thinking that God wants us in church, we may go to church. If we consider that being in church is particularly worshiping God we should be at the church service. If we think that God wants us to take part in the church program, we should do it if we think that is what God wants. We will subscribe and give a dollar to impress God if that's what we think God wants. We return thanks at the table, and have an occasional prayer with our family if we actually think that this is what He wants from us. If we should walk by any place where someone is holding out a tambourine for a gift we will give something, if we think that is what God wants us to do. Without disparaging any of these acts, the truth of the matter is that our actions will be according to what we think of God.

But if we look upon our Lord Jesus Christ we will think of God as seen in Jesus Christ. "He that hath seen the Son, hath seen the Father" (paraphrase of John 14:9). When we know about the Lord Jesus Christ and God we will know that what God wants is each one of us personally. Then after He has us, He wants to use us to manifest to men the grace of God. Pure religion and undefiled before God and the Father is this: that we do His will in visiting and helping the poor. We are going to keep ourselves clean and undefiled from any kind of selfishness. We will keep ourselves unspotted from the world by denying ourselves. In this way we can expect the blessing of God.

Chapter 13

HAVE NO RESPECT FOR PERSONS

> My brethren, have not the faith of our Lord Jesus Christ, the Lord of glory, with respect of persons. For if there come unto your assembly a man with a gold ring, in goodly apparel, and there come in also a poor man in vile raiment; and ye have respect to him that weareth the gay clothing, and say unto him, Sit thou here in a good place; and say to the poor, Stand thou there, or sit here under my footstool: are ye not then partial in yourselves, and are become judges of evil thoughts? (James 2:1-4).

James is emphasizing that as far as all believers are concerned, human judgment must never affect the public worship of God. In the first verse James is expressing a general principle. In verses two and three he uses an illustration with a comment in verse four. It is not hard to get his point. Our difficulty is not simply to see just what James has in mind, but rather to apply it to ourselves.

In our worship services, when we are bowing down before the Lord Jesus Christ, the Lord of glory, we must never exercise our personal feelings with respect of persons. Our human judgment must not enter into the way in which we conduct ourselves in a public worship service. Public worship is a corporate act, to which different people have come together for one purpose. As we worship in the fellowship of other people, we must never allow our personal appraisal of others to enter into our judgment or into our actions. All of us are just repentant sinners who believe in the Lord of glory. Noticing the outward appearance of a fellow worshiper has no place in a church service.

It is no doubt true that in this mixed world there are some

people we find it hard to like personally. There are some people that we do not associate with as personal companions. Actually, day by day, they are not among our friends. They may not do the things we do. They may not live on our side of the street. They may not dress as we dress. But if these people want to come to worship God with us, we must accept them into our fellowship without showing any personal preference in our conduct.

What gives the worship service its meaning is that it is the worshiping of God that is being carried on. The name of God lifts the whole experience to its true significance. So it is not really *our* service, it is actually *His*. God is no respecter of persons, and calls all men to Him. We ought not to presume to act as if this were our own affair: it is His, and He makes all welcome.

James writes on to give an illustration (I have paraphrased slightly): "If there come into your assembly" — into your gathering of Christians, "a man wearing a gold ring and goodly apparel" — a person wearing finely tailored clothes who has evidence of means, "and there come in also a poor man in vile raiment" — in shabby clothing. (This need not mean that they are dirty but that they are inexpensive or even cheap.) "And you have respect to him that weareth the gay clothing. And you say to the poor man stand thou there, and sit here under my footstool." Since we do not know the inner differences between these people, we look at their clothing and decide that the one over here is obviously more important than the one over there. Because of the way one man was dressed we treat him with respect. We ask him to sit in a good place. Then we offer the poor a lesser place.

James writes against such conduct. He asks, "Are you not then partial in yourselves and become judges of evil thought?" When in our thinking we make human distinctions by class, and base our judgment on appearance, we are guilty of doing an evil thing. We have shown bad judgment on a wrong basis. God does not act in this manner.

In our own family we had two sons who grew up together, passed through high school and then entered college. Both were in the service. One was in the Navy, the other was in the Marines. Later they began to prepare for their first employment in the business world. I should say that as long as they were in our home, as boys, they had to get along without much money. Money was pretty scarce with us.

As it happened the younger of the two completed enough of his work at the University to obtain a very well paying job, in which he was receiving a goodly sum of money. He had the disposition to tithe, so now he had money to give. At this particular time his work took him to California. Once when he came home on a visit, I overheard the two boys talking in their room. One said to the other, "You know when you have money people treat you differently." His brother said, "Well, I wouldn't know about that, I've never had any." So the first one said, "I'll tell you something that happened not long ago: I was in a California city, hunting around for a church to attend. I went to a certain church. I was a stranger and an usher saw me and pointed to an empty seat and I went and sat down. Well that day as it happened, I had some tithe money to give. So I put a twenty dollar bill in the plate. The next Sunday I went back to the same church, and you know what? Two ushers showed me to a seat, and I could almost have laughed out loud." Hearing them talk, I chuckled to myself. Just imagine the difference a twenty dollar bill can make.

James warns us that when we are worshiping God we must be very careful lest our personal human judgment affect our conduct. I would not think this would mean that we should disown all natural feeling. It would seem natural for those who come from a certain part of the country to group together. In many large cities it is not surprising to find whole congregations of people coming from a certain place. We would expect people of the same trades to group together. Farmers, for example, would tend to be with farmers. Mechanics will tend to be with mechanics, and mill workers pretty much tend to be with other mill workers. Financiers would tend to be with people who work in finance.

This would be a natural grouping according to vocation.

The same principle is true in age groups. It is not unusual to find young people being together and older people going together; men going together and women going together. Such groupings are not uncommon. They are natural, too.

The same would be true of nationality. There would be a French-speaking congregation over here and a German or an Italian congregation over there. Such groupings might reflect only natural differences. But differences based on human nature must not be brought into public worship services.

Whoever comes to worship God in a church, which is named by His name, must be accepted by us. He must feel free to come into our service and be seated and take his place like anyone else. Some of our old denominations are most careful in treating everyone, poor and rich the same way. God will honor them for this. It is not a wholesome thing, to favor those who are rich or those who speak our language, or those whom we know.

This truth is very important in our day and time. There have been disturbances throughout our country because people of different races have come together to take part in the public worship of God. Sometimes it has been difficult to keep this issue clear because of local controversy.

James would seem to imply we cannot possibly close our place of worship to anyone who wants to come. Even if we are at a disadvantage, "whosoever will may come" is basic. God is no respecter of persons. If we are going to indicate something comes from God, our hearts must be inclined to do it God's way. We must offer ourselves to Him and ask His guidance in these matters.

Chapter 14

AVOID FAVORING THE RICH

Hearken, my beloved brethren, Hath not God chosen the poor of this world rich in faith, and heirs of the kingdom which he hath promised to them that love him? But ye have despised the poor. Do not rich men oppress you, and draw you before the judgment seats? Do not they blaspheme that worthy name by the which ye are called? If ye fulfill the royal law according to the scripture, Thou shalt love thy neighbour as thyself, ye do well: but if ye have respect to persons, ye commit sin, and are convinced of the law as transgressors (James 2:5-9).

Have we ever thought that we could be rich apart from having money? The words "poor" and "rich" do not necessarily mean that we are without money, or that we have money. There are other ways of being poor or being rich than owning or not owning property.

We say a person is rich when he is fortunate. This could be a matter of money and it often is. If someone has enough money to give him an advantage over other people, he could be called rich. But one could be called rich in family. There are some people who are rich in their family association. It could be culture. We could be born in a certain country, among a certain class of people that could give us an advantage over others. We could be rich in that way. You can be rich in friends. There are the friends you choose, and oftentimes there are friends which we inherit, people who are friends of our family. Some people are rich in physical strength. They have health and strength and vitality that really gives them a big advantage over other people. Some people are rich in intellectual gifts. In the same way social standing and having friends or relations who are influential, can have distinct advantages. Any of these things could make us rich.

In the book of James, verses 5 - 9, we find that James is writing to us as if we were Christians. In this matter of riches, he admonishes us, he advises and he urges us to be very careful that we do not fall into the snare of favoring fortunate people. Favoring rich people often could mean favoring ungodly people. This would not be true to our profession.

I can remember being at a church conference some years ago when I overheard some people talking. One person was telling another how to get along in church affairs. He used this expression: "Well, I'll tell you one thing, you're going to have to pet the big dog." That thing has often come to my mind. Every now and again, when I see some people going around in church affairs, I think to myself: there's one of them trying to pet the big dogs. Jesus would point out how unlike the Lord Jesus such conduct actually is.

In this portion of his letter, James is still writing about the matter of making distinctions between people according to their outward appearance, according to their outward standing. When he speaks to his readers, he calls them, "beloved brethren." He wants them to understand that even though he will speak sternly and sharply to them it is for their own good. He means well by them. Above all else he wants them to be blessed. "Hath not God chosen the poor of this world rich in faith?" Let us search our hearts as we ask ourselves if we are ready to know who the poor of this world are. It cannot mean those who have money. There are some people without money that are actually rich, and others who are wealthy from a human standpoint, who are poor, so very poor.

Sometimes when we go into a rich person's home, we can feel the tension that is there. We become aware of the jealousy, the envy and pride that exists. We sense the arrogance in that home, and we know that we are moving among people who are actually stark poor. They do not realize that they do not have a thing that makes for blessing. James is writing to Christians everywhere. How often many of us who want to be counted as Christians are not really giving ourselves over to it. We are not working at it. We are not playing the game. Actually James is addressing us. He is writing to us because it is true that God has chosen those who say they are poor. In His Sermon on the Mount, our Lord Jesus said, "Blessed are the poor in spirit: for theirs is the kingdom of heaven" (Matthew 5:3). Such people are poor in spirit, in the sense that they know their own inadequacy. They know that they are not fit nor good enough: they realize that with all their wisdom they do not know much. To these people we could say that they are blessed.

We could say that those people are strong who realize that with all their strength, they could not prolong their life a single day. These people also know that as far as their friends are concerned, that between God and man, between themselves and God, their friends cannot help them there. They need the Lord. They are poor in spirit. These are people who are not necessarily poor as far as this world is concerned. They reckon themselves poor, but they are rich in faith. "And heirs of the kingdom which he hath promised to them that love him? But ye have despised the poor" (verse 5, 6). James warns us of the human tendency to look down on these who are not proud, who do not strut. Deep down we may know that we are not much. Shall we live out this actual fact and have people look down on us? Or shall we put on a big front, so that people will look up to us? This is something each one of us must decide for himself. This is a test each one of us must face.

"Ye have despised the poor. Do not rich men oppress you, and draw you before the judgment seat?" These are blunt words. James would have us realize that it is quite customary for the rich and fortunate to put pressure on the poor and unfortunate. Those who have wealth and family and culture, those who are physically strong or personally beautiful, or of high social standing, actually look down on the less fortunate and treat them as though they were of no account.

Speaking of the rich among Christians James goes on to say, "Do not they blaspheme that worthy name by which ye are called?" (verse 7). This does not mean that they use profanity against God. It means that by their conduct they bring shame upon the name of the Lord Jesus Christ, that worthy name by which they are called. These words apply directly to rich folks who are members of the church. These rich Christians often bring disrepute upon the name of Jesus Christ: they live in ornate luxury. They spend endless money to have everything their hearts desire. They spend money lavishly upon themselves but are sharp and close and careful when it comes to giving to the Lord's work. All this brings blasphemy on the name of the Lord Jesus Christ. Their arrogance causes other people to take offense at their unChristlike conduct. When we read these words and search our own hearts in this matter, most of us admit that much of the money we spend on our homes, on our clothes and our personal adornment could have been used for proclaiming the Gospel.

God sees how we act toward other people. He knows how we feel about them. May we walk in the way of our Lord Jesus Christ, who gave Himself for us. This is the way of blessing.

Chapter 15

THE MEANING OF THE LAW

"For whosoever shall keep the whole law, and yet offend in one point, he is guilty of all. For he that said, Do not commit adultery, said also, Do not kill. Now if thou commit no adultery, yet if thou kill, thou art become a transgressor of the law. So speak ye, and so do, as they that shall be judged by the law of liberty. For he shall have judgment without mercy, that hath showed no mercy; and mercy rejoiceth against judgment" (James 2:10-13).

James was eager that all Christians should receive the full blessing of God. In the preceding study he discusses a very common and practical problem about dealing with people. How should Christians treat the various classes of people who come into the public worship service? He made it very plain that no distinction should be made between the people who are prominent and the people who are not prominent. Nor should Christians ever make a distinction between people who have many friends and the folks who have no friends at all. James wanted believers to escape the snares of being impressed by the rich or of bowing down to the fortunate.

We do well to keep in mind that when James wrote this way it was for the sole purpose of making Christians understand how they may be blessed. He is not writing to show people how to be saved. In all generations, and everywhere, God's message has been, "Whosoever will may come, and whosoever cometh shall in no wise be cast out." All may be saved in just one way: those who accept the Lord Jesus Christ as Saviour will be saved. Almighty God will save our souls and this will establish our relationship with Him. Having been saved it should follow that we grow in grace and in knowledge. We should mature as believers and bear fruit to the glory of God. It is most important that we as Christians bear fruit in order that the Lord Jesus might be pleased: that the Almighty might be pleased with us and that we might be blessed. The blessing of God upon us will depend upon our response, on the way in which we act out the will of God. And this is what James had in mind.

James points out how very important it is for us to understand how to deal with those who are the strong and fortunate ones in our Christian community. This is something which we might almost miss. Actually it is being missed so often in our day. Throughout the length and breadth of the land in church after church, and company after company of Christian believers, we find the tendency to bow down and appreciate the folks that are rich. These are the ones who are elected to office. These are the ones who are most frequently given important responsibilities. But James would have us be on guard against such conduct not becoming to a Christian.

I lived for years on the campus of church supported institutions, and I found that it was a foregone conclusion that the bright student, the smart student, the brilliant student, would be given all the favors. To me it was a travesty, in a sense, upon equity and fair play to see something like this. The student who was brilliant, whose mind was moving easily and freely through the material, did not have to work for the good grades he was getting. Such a student would be given a scholarship. The faculty would arrange to give him money so that he could study without having to work for his expenses. The other student had to work hard for what he received in any subject. He had to dig, and study hard to be able to grasp his prescribed subjects in his studies. If he lacked funds he had to work his way through school. We did not give him any scholarship because we said that he was not smart. This seemed to me then, and even to this day, so contrary to the spirit of the Gospel of the Lord Jesus Christ. It seemed to me that Jesus would have given the favor and the advantage to the poor, to the man who had trouble because he would be the man that needed to be helped.

James writes further, "For whosoever shall keep the whole law, and yet offend in one point, he is guilty of all." These words of James are a warning to all of us. We may be honest and careful in our conduct, we may be sincere and truthful, we may witness to other people and keep various aspects of the law, we may be respectful toward those in authority over us, considerate of our equals, and charitable to the poor. All these things could be true of us as Christians; yet if we actually endorse and favor a person because he is rich, whether in money or prestige or fame, we stand in grave danger of transgressing the law of God. We may still be judged a sinner before God.

As James points out so plainly, it is not necessary to be crude to be a sinner. Believers do not have to be vicious. All in the world it takes to be a sinner is to offend in one point. In this connection we are reminded of a man who tried to put a good front on everything. One day someone said to him, "Well, I see that you have a flat tire." He said, "Yes, it's flat, but just in one place — at the bottom." We may feel that this is a light way to illustrate a point but isn't that the way it is with many of us? We stand up so well except at the bottom. We are flat in one place. It makes us think about a balloon when it is pricked. We need to prick but one tiny hole, and that's the end of the balloon. So it is with many of us. One sin in the sight of God, places us in the state of the sinner that James is speaking about.

Many years ago a man used an illustration. He was speaking of a certain group of people, a regiment in the British army. The only way a man could join this regiment was to be 5′ 11″ in height. The man who was 5′ 11½″ or 5′ 10″ could not get in. It took exactly 5′ 11″ to get in. That is the way it is with rules and regulations. That is the way it is with the law of God. The overall, total picture James gives us here is clear. It does not matter how sure we may be that we are serving God in many different ways. James is very sober in saying that if we miss in one point we are missing the real spirit of the whole thing. In other words, we must not make a difference between people because of their circumstances. We dare not make a difference between people because they are fortunate or because they are poor. All this is a sin in the sight of God.

In verse 12 we read, "So speak ye, and so do, as they that shall be judged by the law of liberty." The law of liberty is the way we go when we are free. We may ask, why are we free? In what sense do we have liberty? Every Christian person has liberty. When the Lord Jesus Christ died, and was buried and rose from the dead, He opened the way for us to believe in Him. He will raise us from the dead in the newness of life, when we are crucified and buried with Him and when we are one hundred per cent yielded to Him. Because we are His, we are free. We have the law of liberty. We are free in the sense that no one can hold regulations over us. We are actually free to do as we please. Since we are free to do as we please, God looks closely at what we are pleased to do. "For he shall have judgment without mercy, that hath showed no mercy" (verse 13). When we show no mercy we do not have the grace of God in our hearts. We will certainly be judged if we are without mercy. "And mercy rejoiceth against judgment" (verse 13). If we have the mercy of God in our hearts, we do not fear His judgment.

Here we might profitably look at I John 4:18: "There is no fear in love; but perfect love casteth out fear: because fear hath torment. He that feareth is not made perfect in love." "Perfect love" occurs when love is activated in conduct. Perfect love is carried out in doing good to other people. If from the bottom of our hearts we actually are disposed to help other people and do them good, we will not be in danger of judgment. If we go out actually helping others we can be sure that God will help us. He would have us be very clear in our minds on this whole matter of being careful not to favor the rich or the poor, that we should look upon men as Christ looked upon them. He made no distinctions. He was no respecter of persons when He gave Himself for all.

Chapter 16

FAITH WITHOUT WORKS IS DEAD

What doth it profit, my brethren, though a man say he hath
faith, and have not works? can faith save him? If a brother or
sister be naked, and destitute of daily food, and one of you
say unto them, Depart in peace, be ye warmed and filled; notwithstanding ye give them not those things which are needful
to the body; what doth it profit? Even so faith, if it hath not
works, is dead, being alone (James 2:14 - 17).

Christians believe that God works His will in the lives of all
who commit themselves to the Lord Jesus Christ. According to
His promise, God's grace is operative in believers moving them
into His will by the will of Jesus Christ. This is the relationship
that actually exists between believers and God. James writes to
be helpful by showing the way to be fruitful in this relationship
with God. When believers want to do the will of God, they often
find it hard to separate their own thoughts and ideas from God's
thoughts. This matter needs discussion and explanation so that
Christians can act intelligently in response to God.

James raises the question "though a man say he hath faith,
and have not works, can faith save him?" There is a basic truth
underlying all that he has in mind: ". . . whatsoever a man
soweth, that shall he also reap" (Galatians 6:7). No one can
question this. It is what a man plants that will determine what
he is going to harvest. When a man goes into his garden and
puts beans into the ground, we do not need to guess what he
is going to get out of the ground. We know that if he gets
anything out of the ground it will be beans. He planted beans
and he will harvest beans. This is just as true in spiritual matters. James makes it very plain that we must keep in mind

that whatsoever we sow that shall we also reap. We must be careful to avoid thinking that whatsoever we say will bring results. Saying is cheap. It's sowing that counts.

James then raises another question in this matter: what do we mean when we say we believe in the Lord Jesus Christ? When a person believes in the Lord Jesus Christ he accepts Christ alone as Leader, as Master, and Teacher. Christ is the Head, the Author and Finisher of our faith. When a man truly believes he is yielded to obey the Lord Jesus Christ in all the issues of living.

The particular case in point that James brings up for discussion involves the believer's conduct with other believers. James instructs us in our treatment of other believers, especially the poor. He brings out the fact that we ought to treat the poor as our Lord treated the poor. Since believing means obeying we can expect that He will not lead us to do differently than He did. As the Father sent Him, so He sends us. What He came to do, and what He did when He was here, is the very thing He will move us to do. There is no question about that. We know that the Lord Jesus Christ never turned away anyone in need, so it would not be right for us to turn anyone away. Our Lord Jesus Christ played no favorites in people. He showed mercy to all, and so it follows that I ought to play no favorites in people, but should do good to all men.

This same truth can be seen in other ways. For instance, in our giving to the Lord's work, we would say that when we are believers we will give to the Lord's work. The Lord Jesus gave everything He had. He gave Himself. If we say that we believe in the Lord Jesus Christ, and we do not give to the poor, we are not true. This would not be honest, if we said that we believed in the Lord and then did not help others. This actually sounds ridiculous and would certainly be a deceitful claim. Believing in the Lord Jesus Christ who gave Himself in His mission, would certainly lead Christians to support missions.

The same principle would be true in the matter of prayer. Could we honestly say that we believed in the Lord Jesus Christ if we do not pray, or we never worship God? Since believing is obeying, Christians will want to do what their Lord would lead them to do. He spent time in prayer, so surely He would lead His followers to spend time in prayer and worship.

Because this matter is so important James presents arguments to clarify his point. "What does it profit, my brethren, though a man say he hath faith, and have not works? Can faith save him?" The "works" James has in mind is the consequence that believing will lead into. What James is saying is that if a man is a believer and does not produce anything, something is missing. If there are no results in conduct, if believing in God does not make a difference in living, something is wrong. "Can faith save him?" By this James means, can faith alone save him if there has been no change in the actions of that man such as the sharing of his goods with the poor?

If a Christian says that he believes, has it made any difference in his conduct? Has his faith changed him or is he just as selfish as before? Just saying that he believes will not produce any change in his character. There will actually be no change in him unless he yields himself into the will of the Lord Jesus Christ. When He saves a man, that man will be different. He will have the attitude of our Lord Jesus Christ with reference to the poor, because His will is now operative in him.

James writes on to give a concrete illustration in regard to the poor. "If a brother or sister be naked, and destitute of daily food, and one of you say unto them, Depart in peace, be ye warmed and filled; notwithstanding ye give them not those things which are needful to the body; what doth it profit?" James is pointing out that just saying, "be ye warmed and filled," and then not giving the poor what they need, amounts to less than nothing. When he discussed the treatment of the poor who came to worship services, James made it clear that Christians must treat all men alike. Believers must not make a distinction in where they are seated, nor how they are received at the church door. If Christians treat them differently, if they pay special attention to one person and none to another person, their conduct will condemn them before God.

James then pressed his point: "Even so faith, if it hath not works, is dead, being alone." That is to say, that faith, if it does not result in obedience to the will of God, is faith without works. Believing means yielding to the will of His Father. When

I yield to the will of God through the Lord Jesus, there will be a difference in my actions. It will follow that I will be walking in a different way. If I say I believe but there is no change in my ways, then my believing is dead. It's like a seed that never grew.

What then does it mean when we say we believe in the Lord Jesus Christ? Do we have any idea of how Jesus Christ obeyed His Father, how He lived, how He died, how He was buried, and how He rose from the dead? Do we have in mind how Jesus Christ appeared before people after His resurrection, how He ascended into heaven, how He is now at the right hand of God the Father, how He is praying for us, and how He will come again to live with us? All this is included when we say that we believe in the Lord Jesus Christ. As He lived, yielded to God to do His will, so we must yield ourselves to do His will. If anyone were to ask us: "Who do you think you are?" we would reply: "By the grace of God we are members of the Body of Christ."

When we have an image in our hearts and minds of how Jesus suffered because He was doing the will of His Father, we would be inclined to do the will of our Father even if we should suffer. We would be walking in His way. Believing in Him means surrendering to God. It means that we will deny ourselves — that we will seek to win others to be saved. Only then is our believing really a matter of faith in Jesus Christ. When we live in faith we will do these things that Jesus did. Otherwise, if our believing does not lead us His way to follow in His way, to do the things Christ did, James would say that what we call our faith, is actually dead.

Chapter 17

FAITH ALONE IS NOT VALID

Yea, a man may say, Thou hast faith, and I have works: show me thy faith without thy works, and I will show thee my faith by my works. Thou believest that there is one God; thou doest well: the devils also believe, and tremble. But wilt thou know, O vain man, that faith without works is dead? (James 2: 18 - 20).

The New Testament doctrine which is known to everyone who has the Gospel in mind is: "We are saved by faith. We are saved through faith. We are saved in faith." The Apostle Paul writes, "By grace are ye saved through faith . . . " (Ephesians 2: 8). In the book of Hebrews we read, "Without faith it is impossible to please him . . . " (11:6). It is by believing, through believing and in believing that a soul is brought into the will of God. This is hard to describe. It is easy to be misled, because believing is so invisible. We believe in God, but we have not seen Him. When we believe in the Word of God, we believe in certain promises that we have not seen as yet. So it is important to examine this whole matter of faith and believing.

James says as clearly as he possibly can, that we who are Christians are in danger. We are in danger of falling into a snare and error. When we think that it is enough to say that we have faith, this is not true. It is only as we can say that we are yielded to God and obey Him that we have faith. James puts this warning in rather strong language. He writes in a way which makes our hearts bow down before God as we listen to his words.

James illustrates what he has in mind. He points out that a

man may come to us and say, "You claim you have faith. I have
something to show you. I have actually done certain works.
That is to say, I have responded to God in my personal actions.
There are certain things about my conduct that are changed,
because I have faith in God. I pray to God, and I give to the
Lord's work. Because I have faith in God I count all men to be
His creatures and souls for whom Christ Jesus died. Because
I have faith in God, I tell other people about the Lord Jesus
Christ, and try to show them by my concern for their welfare
that God cares about them. Thus they may be inclined to listen
and so to hear the Gospel preached and be saved. I do these
things because I have faith in God. Now, you say you have faith.
What do you have to show for it? How would I know that you
have faith? If you watch me and look at what I do, you will see
that I show you my faith by my works."

James is saying in effect that works should be evidence of our
faith. If we claim that we have planted beans in our garden, the
best way to prove that statement is to have some beans growing
there. On the other hand, if we say that we have planted beans
and have nothing but bare ground, we have no evidence to show
that we planted anything. This is what James means. Nothing
intricate, nothing hard to follow. When we say we have faith
we must show some consequences of having yielded to God.
The works that follow real faith are not works of our own.
We cannot talk about doing works in our own strength. We talk
of doing certain things because we believe. This gives us a clear
testimony about our faith.

James writes on to emphasize his idea: "Thou believest there
is one God; thou doest well: the devils also believe, and tremble."
This is one of the sharpest and most severe words in the New
Testament on the whole subject of faith. James is saying, you
do not impress me when you say there is a God. The devils
believed that Jesus of Nazareth was in reality the Christ. Actually, believing in God only distinguishes a man from a fool.
"The fool hath said in his heart, There is no God" (Psalm 14:1).
Anyone who has any sense knows better than that.

Among such people, who believe that there is one God, this
is the proper question to be raised, "Since you believe in God
and in His law, and you know that you are a sinner in the sight

of God, what are you going to do?" Christians know that the Gospel is the answer and the cure for every sinner, "For God so loved the world, that he gave his only begotten Son, that whosoever believeth in him should not perish, but have everlasting life" (John 3:16). James points out that if I really believe this wonderful promise of God, I should be able to show evidence of yieldedness to God. I should indicate by my conduct that the mind of Christ is being worked out in me.

Sometimes "faith" is difficult to understand. We might find it helpful to understand about faith if we would consider the illustration about swallowing. We could readily say, a man lives because he swallows. That sounds all right, but after we think about it a bit, we know right away that we live if we swallow food. We certainly won't live if we just chew. It is swallowing food that keeps us alive. We could carry this illustration on a little further and say, only when we swallow food will we be kept alive. Swallowing poison would kill us even though the swallowing process is the same. Swallowing clean food and swallowing poison do not differ except for the result: life or death.

Believing the truth and believing a lie are very much the same kind of believing. It is a good deal like walking on planks across a creek. If there were two planks crossing a stream of water, we will assume that one of these planks is sound. The other one is unsound and will break. All we can do is walk. If we walk on the one that will hold us we'll cross over. If we walk on the other, it will break and we will fall into the creek. We fell into the creek because we walked on a plank. In the other case we got across because we walked on a plank. Walking on the plank was the same in both cases. We just walked on different planks.

This same truth was seen in the previous illustration. When we swallow food we live. When we swallow poison we die. We swallow truth and we can be saved. We swallow error and we can be lost. It is what we swallow that really feeds the body. And it is what we believe from the Word of the Almighty God that can really save our souls.

Faith must be operative in our lives, if it is going to be real. Our faith is going to have to function because without works our faith is dead. Faith is not tangible. Faith is not a liquid. It is not a perfume. It is not a kind of mist. Faith is a descriptive term which designates the response of the heart and will to God, by yielding to His promises and actually putting trust in God. To have faith in God, we need to be acquainted with His promises. We need to trust in Him, in His will, and in His power. We must know that He will do what He has promised. We must commit ourselves to Him in obedience. All this together is what the Bible means by faith. In other words, when we say that we believe, we must always include that believing is yielding ourselves into the will of God, because we know God and trust Him. We yield to Him and seek to do His will.

In the book of Hebrews, chapter 11 is the great chapter of faith. Here we can read of a number of great men of faith. "By faith Abel offered a more excellent sacrifice than Cain . . ." (paraphrase of verse 4). We see that Abel made a sacrifice. "By faith Abraham came out of his father's country into a land that was new to him" (paraphrase of verse 8). We see that he came out. "By faith Moses refused to be called the son of Pharaoh's daughter, and chose rather to suffer affliction with the people of God for a season" (paraphrase of verses 24, 25). All these examples indicate that faith was operative in a tangible action of some sort. This is a very real challenge to us. We must fully realize that if our faith does not move us to yield ourselves to the will of God, if it has no consequences, it is dead.

These stern, frank words from James makes us feel that he is digging deep down into our own hearts. He has been telling us that God's blessing will surely follow if we truly yield our wills to His will and obey Him. If however, we are not humble and meek, if we do not let God speak to us, if we do not yield to Him and obey Him, we will not be blessed. It will make no difference how much we say, what we say or how much we talk. God's blessing will not follow.

May God help everyone of us to be yielded into the will of the living God, for only then will we receive His blessing.

Chapter 18

FAITH MADE PERFECT BY WORKS

Was not Abraham our father justified by works, when he had offered Isaac his son upon the altar? Seest thou how faith wrought with his works, and by works was faith made perfect? And the scripture was fulfilled which saith, Abraham believed God, and it was imputed unto him for righteousness: and he was called the Friend of God (James 2:21-23).

Faith is significant only when it promotes action. Faith without action is useless. This is the basic principle for everything everywhere, and it is true in every case. It would be true in the matter of farming. It would be true in the matter of insuring a home. It would be true in the matter of conducting a business. If we say that we have faith in anything and we do nothing about it, our faith does not amount to a thing. Faith without action is useless.

This principle has a deep spiritual meaning when we apply it to our experiences as Christians. Believing in Jesus Christ and being a Christian, is in a sense a means by which we receive that which God has promised. Now a common error is possible here. We may actually believe in and have confidence in something so strongly, and then think that when we say we believe in it, this is enough to make it come to pass. There is a sense in which this is true but there is also another sense in which this is not true. The truth is that God makes things come to pass, and He does this by His own grace.

The grace of God does not operate separately from, or opposite from, the creation He has made. This whole matter of believing needs to be understood something like this: to believe as Christians we must hear and understand what God has said. We must know the promises of God because they are actually a form of the will of God. This is what God will do. Invariably in any promise of God, there is a directive which the Bible calls a commandment. This is the way God deals with us. Nowhere in the Bible does it imply that God is going to give, without any response from us. God will not give to us so that we can go and squander and indulge ourselves on our own. That is not God's way. God will give us certain things and we must respond and follow through. What God gives to us is related to what He wants us to do. Every promise of God includes basically some commandment of God, the obeying of which actually is believing.

Let us once again consider a garden as an illustration in this matter of believing. Not one of us can produce beans apart from God operating through the processes of nature. No man can grow beans. God can and will grow beans. Now the circumstances under which the beans are produced are in the will of God. It is true that there must be soil and water and proper temperature. There are many practical, reasonable, sensible conditions that must be met for the beans to grow. Now all of these conditions do not make the beans grow. God makes them grow, but He does this according to these conditions which are in a sense His will. Any one of us can raise beans if he is willing to follow God's explicit conditions in this matter.

Suppose that we were to go out into our back yards and throw beans on frozen ground in order to raise beans. Throwing beans on frozen ground is not obeying God's commandment about beans. We must realize that there is a certain basic directive in the very nature of things. When we follow through on that we can be sure that "whatsoever a man soweth, that shall he also reap" (Galatians 6:7).

James uses an Old Testament story to illustrate this profound truth. He draws attention to Abraham himself, and shares a most important insight on faith. "Was not Abraham our father justified by works, when he offered Isaac his son upon the altar?" These words, "justified by works," are a startling statement. We can be amazed by them. The Apostle Paul in his epistles to the Ephesians, Galatians and Romans has stated clearly that we are justified by faith. In the context in which Paul is discussing this truth, it is true that we are justified by faith. Now we must open our hearts and minds and let James speak to us. "Was not Abraham our father justified by works, when he offered Isaac his son upon the altar? Seest thou how faith wrought with his works, and by works was faith made perfect? And the scripture was fulfilled which saith, Abraham believed God, and it was imputed to him for righteousness and he was called the Friend of God."

In the context where James is presenting this truth there is a most profound and important statement. The word, "justified," means to be made "just." This word "just" is an adjective that describes a person as being acceptable before God. Paul argued that we are made acceptable before God when we believe in Him. James argues that our believing in God includes responding to God and obeying God. Paul would not discount this at all. This word "works" does not mean, works apart from faith. These are not "works" we do in our own strength. These are not works done by a human being in himself or in his own wisdom. These are the works in which we respond and yield to the will of God as we endeavor to serve Him in obedience.

Was not Abraham our father justified — made acceptable before God (by works — by responding to God) — when he had offered Isaac his son upon the altar? This is what God asked Abraham to do and Abraham obeyed God. His faith was his response. This is faith in action. In verse 22 we read, "Seest thou how faith wrought with his works, and by works was faith made perfect?" In other words faith operated in him and led him to obey God. ". . . by works was faith made perfect?" The words "made perfect" do not mean that Abraham's faith needed improving or correcting. There was nothing wrong with Abraham's faith. Made perfect means that it was fulfilled. It was brought through to completion. Here faith bore fruit and thus the Scripture was fulfilled.

"Abraham believed God." What should this mean to us when we say that we believe in the Lord Jesus Christ? What can we do to fulfill this faith? We search our heart for the answer and we can find it there. We realize that much is implied in the words, "I believe in the Lord Jesus Christ." First of all we confess that we are sinners and we repent of our sins. We must deny ourselves and commit ourselves to our Lord and Saviour Jesus Christ. Then we will realize that we are no longer our own, and we will earnestly seek God's will for us.

We realize that action must follow real faith. When Sunday comes around we will endeavor to be in the worship service of our church if we believe in God. As the days come and go we will read the Bible. We will pray because we believe in God. Suppose I say I believe in the Holy Spirit. When I say this I mean that I am conscious of the Holy Spirit and have received the Holy Spirit. This is the significance of saying that faith is fulfilled. The Scripture is fulfilled by my response to God in obedience to His will.

Chapter 19

RAHAB WAS JUSTIFIED

> Ye see then how that by works a man is justified, and not by
> faith only. Likewise also was not Rahab the harlot justified
> by works, when she had received the messengers, and had sent
> them out another way? (James 2:24, 25).

In the book of James, we are impressed with the clear logic
and reasonableness of the whole matter of Christian living. This
book is not an involved argument or explanation about some
point of doctrine. It is, rather, a series of practical applications
of truth to specific problems. In the latter part of the second
chapter, James takes up one of these problems: the problem of
faith. The life and the faith of the Christian is beset by many
perils and dangers just as a garden is beset with weeds.

James has been warning Christians to avoid the snare of thinking that when we say that we believe we have done enough.
Saying we believe and *doing* His will are very different. A parable told by the Lord Jesus Christ clearly illustrates this point.
A certain man had two sons. The father told both of them to
go to the field and work. One said that he would, but he didn't
go. The other son said he would not go, but he went. The
Lord Jesus asked this question of the Pharisees: "Which one
did the will of his father; which one was actually obedient to
the father?" They all answered, "The one who went of course."
James wants to emphasize above all else the importance of the
way we act in response to the will of God. Our actions will
validate our claim that we belong to Him.

When Paul wrote the Christians in Rome and Galatia about
being justified, he was speaking about being made just before

God. He was speaking about our being made acceptable in the sight of God by the death of Jesus Christ.

James uses the word justified with a different emphasis than Paul did. When James writes about justification he is referring to the experience of a person being made acceptable before God in actual practice.

It is one thing to be cleared from all guilt because Jesus Christ died for us. It is another thing to have our way of life acceptable in the sight of God. This does not mean that we will be sinless. It does not mean that we will have a perfect score. It means that when we are definitely yielded to God, we can have an acceptable attitude.

James gives another illustration of being justified by responding to God. He asks the question "was not Rahab the harlot justified by works, when she received the messengers, and had sent them out another way?" This question refers back to an incident in Israel's history during the days of Joshua. This is the experience of the two spies who came into the house of Rahab in the city of Jericho. They were representatives of Israel who were the people of God. Rahab believed that the Israelites were the people of God. She believed in God, and she also believed that He would actually help Israel take the whole city of Jericho. So she befriended the two spies. She hid them up in the roof of her house and covered them with flax straw. When some soldiers of the city came at the command of the king to search for the spies, they could not find them. After the soldiers were gone she brought them down from their place on the roof. She told them which way the soldiers had gone, and sent them on another way.

Later we read in the account of how the walls of Jericho did fall down, and how the city was captured. Rahab and her family were spared because she had hung a scarlet thread out of her window according to her instructions from the two spies. James is saying that she was spared because first of all she had befriended the spies. Secondly she had hung that red thread from her window. In other words, she did certain things. She did not just sit idle expecting God to do it. Because she believed in God, she responded to the situation. She hid the spies because she believed in God. She hung the red cord out of the window because she believed God would give Jericho into the hand of Israel.

What should a Christian do in response to God's call? When he says that he believes in God, he should remember that actions speak louder than words. James is emphasizing the fact that Rahab's faith was the true faith because she acted in line with what she believed.

Christians can apply this truth to themselves. Suppose believers say that they trust in God with regard to their children. This would be a good statement for a Christian: "I believe in God in connection with my children." If this is true, does he show it by following the Word of God in regard to his children? Does he discipline them? Does he remember that when he brings up his children in the way they should go, when they are old, they will not depart from it? He can have in mind that the Word of God will direct him to bring up and train his children in the nurture and admonition of the Lord.

If Christians trust God with regard to their children, do they teach them the Bible? Do they actually teach them what the Bible says? Do they encourage them to pray? Do they set them an example by praying themselves? Do they pray for them? Believers will follow through on all of these things if they believe in God: they will pray for their children. They will teach them the Bible, and take them to Sunday school and church. If they believe in God, they will act according to their convictions.

This is the point that James is emphasizing. When Christians act in line with what they actually believe they can truly expect that what they believe will come to pass. Let them never, for any reason, think that this is just a matter of words. This is something they must think through. What are they actually being asked to do? The answer is clear. Believers must yield themselves to God and put their trust in Him as they obey Him. They must believe in the Lord Jesus Christ and in God's overruling power and protecting care. They must believe that God is actually available to them. He will be on hand when they call unto Him in prayer. In other words they must act according to the way they believe. Then they will have the kind of faith that God can endorse and make fruitful in their lives.

Chapter 20

SO FAITH WITHOUT WORKS IS DEAD

For as the body without the spirit is dead, so faith without works is dead also" (James 2:26).

James writes as a faithful pastor to promote the spiritual growth of new believers. In his epistle James gives practical instructions as to how Christians can keep their lives "free from weeds." Generally speaking when we read his book we get the feeling that his words are to function as a hoe for our personal use in hoeing out the weeds. His words have an actual cleansing power in them. At times when James is so critical in the way he writes, we are almost inclined to think that he is against believers. In reality he wrote his epistle that we as Christians might be fruitful.

We may be sure there is many a child that has at some time or another felt that his mother was dead set against him. He probably resented the way she was also forever asking him to wash his hands. It seemed to him that she was always asking him to comb his hair and to see that his shoes were clean. She seemed to be continually pointing out something that child should do. The truth of the matter was that she wanted her child to learn. She wanted her child to grow up, as a person who understands how to get along with people and thus do well.

There is a profound spiritual truth expressed by the Lord Jesus Christ in John 15:2: ". . . every branch that beareth fruit, he purgeth it, that it may bring forth more fruit." This means that each believer in Christ Jesus who lives and acts in line with his faith will be disciplined. He will be supervised by God in such a way that he may bring forth more fruit. Believers are led through pruning experiences, cutting away dead branches or thinning them out.

In the early part of Chapter 2, James discussed the Christian's attitude toward other believers. He pointed out how natural it is for us to discriminate among men according to their appearance, wealth and tastes. There would be, of course, people we like better because they are like us and we have a lot in common with them. James pointed out that since God is no respecter of persons, we believers in God should not respect persons. This would not be because we want to imitate God. But rather when we follow in His way, and our faith in Him is genuine, His Holy Spirit is operative in us to do His will. In this way our Lord's. manner of dealing with people will come to our thinking. We will find ourselves motivated to act in the will of God, as it is in Jesus Christ. Thus we will not be respecters of persons. On the other hand if we do respect persons, we will then have weeds growing where there should be beans. And it is at this point that James swings a sharp hoe.

In the course of his discussion James warned believers they are in constant danger of failing to act in line with their beliefs, and thus could very well miss the blessing of God. To understand what James had in mind we may consider parents who dedicate their children to the Lord. In some communions of the Christian church children are baptized. In other communions they do not practice the ceremony of baptism, but dedicate the children. Now in the case of parents who bring their children to dedicate them to God, James would raise the question: Did they follow through on the promises they made? They promised that they would bring their children up in the nurture and admonition of the Lord. This would mean that they would read the Bible with the child and bring him to the truth of the Gospel. They promised to pray for them and with them and set them a good example. James would ask have they done any of these things? He would emphasize that it is a dangerous thing to neglect the promises we made before God.

When believers join the fellowship of the church they openly and publicly confess that they believe in the Lord Jesus Christ. They are asked certain questions. One of the questions may be whether they will support the local church. They probably said they would and this no doubt was their intention, but have they been faithful in church attendance? If Christians join a church and then never go to it or share in it, this is an illustration of faith without works.

Christians say that they believe the Bible to be the Holy Word of God, but do they read it? If they say that they believe in the Bible but they do not read it, James would say, "You have faith but you do not live it." The same would be true with reference to prayer. Christians claim that they believe in prayer. Do they just talk about it? Do they believe in prayer and never pray? James would say to us that they were fooling themselves.

Jesus of Nazareth told a parable along this line. He told of the wise and foolish virgins. Ten virgins were watching for their master, but five of them had no oil in their lamps. They had lamps and they were there with the others on time, as it were, but their lamps without oil were useless. They did not act in line with their expectations.

Some years ago in my pastoral experience, I remember being in a certain Sunday school. The Sunday school staff was discussing practical matters about their building. One of the things they brought up was the matter of checking on their fire escape. You know what they found out in that church? They found that while they had a fire escape all right, the doors to the fire escape were locked and no one knew where the keys were! Can you imagine a fire escape with a locked door, and no one knowing where the key is? You'd say, "That's ridiculous." You are right: it is. It is just as ridiculous as it sounds, and just as tragic, too. You'd be surprised how many Christian lives are just like that. They say they believe but they do nothing in line with what they say. Any school boy knows that the finest car in the world needs gas. Every now and again you see some fine car sitting on the highway and it won't run. Why? Out of gas. This reminds us of some Christians. How many there are who are out of gas! They are believers. We do not need to correct them about that, but James reminds them and emphasizes the fact that "The body without the Spirit is dead."

Many years ago my older sister's first baby was still-born. I remember how badly we all felt. A perfectly formed child, with not a single flaw in its organs according to her doctor, but no life. How sad! "Faith without works is dead." This means faith that is not producing anything. Such faith is dead.

Some of us remember how hard it was to start some of our cars in cold weather years ago. We had to crank them to get the engine running. When the oil was stiff and the mechanism was all clogged up, we would jack up one hind wheel, then we could turn the engine over without any trouble. In that way we could get the engine started. Many a time as a boy I have sat in the car at a time that the rear wheels were jacked up off the ground, with the engine running to warm it up. I have thought of that many times since I have become a Christian. The engine was running, all the noise and all the shaking and rattling was there, but the car was not going anywhere. And I have wondered how many Christians are like that! They go through all the motions, all the excitement, they say the right words, they even go to church, but they never apply anything they are saying.

Parents who believe in God should teach the Bible to their children. Believers who profess faith should join the church, attend services and give support. Christians who believe the Bible should read and study the Bible. Christians who believe in prayer should pray, pray, pray.

Chapter 21

THE DANGER IN BEING A TEACHER

> My brethren, be not many masters, knowing that we shall re-
> ceive the greater condemnation. For in many things we offend
> all (James 3:1, 2a).

We know that the whole matter of being a Christian is basically
a matter of believing. Whatever we have in mind as true, whatever we commit ourselves to, as far as our life is concerned,
is what we believe. Believing is certainly an exercise of the will
in committal, but it is first an exercise of the mind. It is a matter
of knowing the promises of God and deciding: I am going to
depend on that — that is what I have chosen for myself. When
we hear some promise of God, and in our hearts we commit ourselves to it, we actually claim that promise for ourselves. This
is believing.

Before we can claim God's promises we must have a willing
frame of mind. We must seek out and know the way of God,
and the will of God, before we can commit ourselves to it. All
of this is involved in believing. None of us was born with the
knowledge needed to become a believer. Such knowledge we
needed to receive apart from ourselves. The problem of receiving
such knowledge in order to have faith is a matter of being involved in learning something. If we are going to learn something,
it must be communicated to us by someone who already knows
it. Thus we would say that if we are going to be Christians,
we need to find out what God has promised to do for us in
Christ Jesus, so that we can believe it.

This is true for everyone! Not only for a scholar in school, not only for someone living in a home. No matter what our calling may be — professional man, business man or laborer — we must learn how to believe. We must learn what God has said He would do. If we are to believe, we need to learn what to believe. We must decide what we are going to believe and then we can truly believe it. For this we need help, we need instruction. Usually someone who knows what to do, and is already committed to believing, should lead us by teaching us. We need a teacher who can share what he knows, who can guide us where he himself is going.

In one sense everyone is always teaching something. Much of it is done informally, but everyone and anyone is teaching something. The children at home learn from grown-up people in the home. They do not go to classes, they do not need books or take notes. They are learning by imitating older people. That is the way a child learns to talk. That is the way a child learns to eat and to dress. A child has to learn everything that it does. If there is a right way to do certain things he must be taught that way by someone who already knows that way of doing.

Some people are designed as teachers. We have teachers in business enterprises as well as in schools and universities. There are people who teach in large factories. They may be called foremen, they may be instructors of one sort or another, but they teach other people what to do.

Normally speaking the name "teacher" is a title of honor. When someone is called a teacher, we feel that he is a bit above the rest of us because he tells us how things should be done. A teacher has a duty to others. We expect certain things from him. When someone is introduced to us, we may be told, "This is Mr. Brown, a teacher." We would at once feel that here is someone we can look up to, someone who can be trusted. We expect to learn from this person who is called teacher.

At the same time a teacher will be criticized more closely than anyone else. The words criticizing and judging mean the same thing. A teacher will be judged more carefully, more precisely than anyone else. Once a person is designated as a teacher, people are inclined to listen to him. This means that he will have special responsibility and this will make a difference in his conduct. This may be what James had in mind when he advised, "My brethren, be not many masters." Here the word "masters" actually means "teachers." In other words, do not take being a teacher as a casual thing. Do not seek to become one. Not many of us should undertake to be teachers, "Knowing that those of us who are teachers, shall receive the greater condemnation" (paraphrase). This is the way James points out that as teachers we will be criticized more closely than anyone else. All Christians should keep this in mind when they consider a place of leadership.

To some extent every Christian is a teacher. Anyone who says, "I am a Christian," stands out in front of other people. In a sense he is calling them to follow him as he goes: "Believe as I believe, do as I do, because I believe in the Lord Jesus Christ, and I am following Him." Every Christian has this responsibility. This makes being a Christian very important, and this is what James is talking about.

This whole idea can well be grasped when we ask, "Should a Sunday school teacher act the same as anyone else?" The answer is simple. When we are named as Sunday school teachers we must be more careful in our conduct than we have ever been before. When we teach Sunday school our class will look up to us, and other people in the church will look to our conduct. A person could say: "Being a Sunday school teacher does not make me perfect." This, of course, is true, but it is also true that when we accepted the place of a Sunday school teacher we assumed a grave responsibility. We stepped out in front. Our conduct now matters to other people.

When a person is asked to serve as an officer of the church, the same truth applies. I was a pastor for a number of years and I know something of the difficulty in getting men to accept the responsibility of a church office. Some people would be willing to accept such a position without accepting any new responsibility. That is not the way to do it. Many times I have gone with a committee to approach a man to ask if he would accept the position of deacon if he were elected. Would he accept the position of elder if we elected him to that position? Often I have heard men say something like this: "Do you expect me to make any change in my way of doing things? If I accept this position of deacon or elder in the church, will it mean a difference in my conduct?" Often a pastor is tempted to say, "Why you're just fine the way you are. People know about you and they have elected you. You are the man they want." I could have said this but it would not have been quite true, not quite good enough. A faithful statement to the man who is about to be elected as an officer of the church would be, "It depends on what you have been doing. The chances are that you will need to make changes in your conduct and in your actions." This would be my answer now to any man who is being asked to accept the office of steward in any church. When we hold a church office we are out in front, we have assumed the responsibility of leadership.

Sometimes we have heard this question about preachers: "Why do preachers act differently from other people? Why can't they be just like anyone else?" Once in a while we see a preacher who tries to be a good mixer and so acts just like everyone else. How do we actually feel when we see a preacher act in this way? I admit that I would feel that he is letting down on something and I would be perfectly right. A preacher need not wear a certain form of apparel, though some do. He does not necessarily need to have a certain style in speech, although it may come to that. But we do expect something different in the conduct of a preacher or a Sunday school teacher. When we look at a Bible class teacher it becomes important to us how he handles the Bible. We might have various ideas in our own minds, but when someone has been named as a minister or a preacher we expect him to be different.

James says one thing that applies to this matter. In James 3:2a he says, "In many things we offend all." These words have been translated like this. "All of us make mistakes." But this does not change the truth that being a leader is a very serious thing. When we shrink from being leaders, when we hesitate about accepting responsibility, we are actually showing some good sense. It is a serious consideration to face. If we love the Lord, and we love His people, we will be willing to take on such responsibility, but we should accept it carefully. We must at all times keep in mind that it is God who called us. He has asked us to lead and He is asking us to be careful. We will need His grace to help us to be faithful.

Chapter 22

A LITTLE CAN DO A LOT

If any man offend not in word, the same is a perfect man, and able also to bridle the whole body. Behold, we put bits in the horses' mouths, that they may obey us; and we turn about their whole body. Behold also the ships, which though they be so great, and are driven of fierce winds, yet they are turned about with a very small helm, whithersoever the governor listeth (James 3:2b-4).

James emphasizes how important little things can be. This is a general truth and the advice James has to give would be good for anyone to follow. Yet the way of life which James describes cannot be, or rather will not be lived by the "natural" man. There is a difference between a natural man and a Christian. By "natural man" we mean anyone without Christ. The difference between the natural man and the Christian has nothing to do with their individual experiences in this world. Both will get wet in the rain. Both of them will get hot in the sun. They will become tired, and hungry. Both have to pay their rent. The natural man has to buy gas for his car, and the Christian has to buy gas for his car. Both have to meet people and deal with them. Their experiences in life are very similar. For this reason the practical advice from James could be used by either.

James has in mind that the way of life which is acceptable to God is the life of a Christian. This life proceeds from surrender to the Lord Jesus Christ. It goes on through self-denial and ends in victory. This life each one of us must accept for himself. There is no other way to share in Christian living. This way was shown in the person of Jesus of Nazareth. He said, "I do nothing of myself. I do all things to please my

Father" (paraphrase of John 8:28, 29). Jesus' total complete surrender to God led Him along the way to Calvary. He went to His death on the cross in obedience to God. Doing the will of God brought Him through death to victory; through the resurrection into the very presence of God. Many sincere persons become confused when they hear about the principles of the Gospel, which we commonly call Christian living. They become confused when they are told to apply these principles in their own lives. They hear the word "self-denial" and ask, "How do we do it? What will it be like to have self-denial?" It simply means to yield in obedience to the will of God.

James illustrates the operation of this principle by bringing up a case in point. He is going to explain this matter of self-denial. He uses as an example "the tongue" — our speech. He involves the whole issue of living by saying, "If a man offend not in word [if we do not say the things we should not say, that is, if we control our speech], the same is a perfect man [a mature person], and also able to bridle the whole body." In other words, anyone that can control his tongue can control himself.

Showing his meaning James uses illustrations to show that although the tongue is small it can be very important. For example, he speaks of the "bit" which is put into horses' mouths — that little piece of steel placed in the mouth of a horse by which he is guided. James points out that although the bit in the mouth of the horse is small, with it the whole horse can be turned. Next, James speaks of a great ship on the sea. Fierce storms drive it through the waves, and yet it can be steered by a small rudder or helm. The rudder is so small that one man can handle it with his hands. With it, the whole ship can be turned.

If James were living today, he might have asked us to consider the automobile weighing a ton or more hurtling down the road. Its steering wheel is small but with it the whole car is turned. Take for instance the light fixtures in a house. James could have used that for an illustration. You can throw one switch and the whole house is dark. Turn that switch on again and the whole house lights up. The ignition switch is small but it controls all the lights. Light fixtures are controlled and can be put off and on by flipping a small button.

We think of a small sum of thirty pieces of silver and find it almost impossible to believe that they were the price of the betrayal of our Lord. Judas, who had been with Jesus for three years and had seen and heard Him, had allowed such a little thing as money to affect him to such an extent.

We think of Mary who brought a box of rare perfume to anoint the Lord. The box itself was small. Yet with this small box of ointment she accomplished a very meaningful act. What a fragrance has come from that act of hers from that day to this.

How often we have begun our day wishing and hoping to live it in the presence of God. We have our house work to do. We have our business responsibilities to carry out. What can we possibly do that would involve our relationship with God? We may say, taking the Bible in our hand and reading a few verses is such a little thing. Ah yes, but when we do it, there is blessing in it. When we take time for prayer it is often only for minutes. It is such a little thing — but when we do, there is blessing in it. When we take part in the singing in our church service, it is such a little thing we do, but there is blessing in it. The same is true with giving. Very seldom do we reach in for money that hurts to give. Yet we give money we could have spent for something we could enjoy. We place it on the collection plate. It seems such a little thing to do, but thank God, with Him there are no little things.

We remember when the Lord Jesus saw the widow coming into the temple with her two mites. They were all she had, "her whole living," but she gave them, she cast them into the collection box. Jesus said to His disciples, "This poor widow hath cast more in, than all they which have cast into the treasury" (Mark 12:43). Her gift was small, but it was great in the eyes of our Lord who looked into her heart and saw her sacrifice. How important little things can be.

Chapter 23

THE TONGUE IS UNRULY

> Even so the tongue is a little member, and boasteth great things. Behold, how great a matter a little fire kindleth! And the tongue is a fire, a world of iniquity: so is the tongue among our members, that it defileth the whole body, and setteth on fire the course of nature; and it is set on fire of hell. For every kind of beasts, and of birds, and of serpents, and of things in the sea, is tamed, and hath been tamed of mankind: but the tongue can no man tame; it is an unruly evil, full of deadly poison (James 3:5-8).

James deals with the practical problem of self control. He is discussing this problem with Christians in order that they may be fruitful, that they may live in such a way that the actual experience as they live day by day, may be blessed. As an example he shows how the control of the whole body may be seen in the way we control our tongues.

James focuses attention on the tongue with good reason. Have we ever considered that the secret of the tongue is in the heart? Do we have in mind that the word "tongue" actually refers to our thoughts, to our inward desires, to our imaginations and in a very real sense to ourselves? All of these various aspects clearly suggest that James is not using the word "tongue" in its physical sense. Have we ever realized that when we think we really talk to ourselves? In other words we are "tongueing" our thoughts over in our minds. This is what we have in mind when James says "the tongue": the inward thoughts of a man.

James is very graphic in his illustrations. "Even so the tongue is a little member, and boasteth great things. Behold, how great a matter a little fire kindleth! And the tongue is a fire, a world

100

of iniquity: so is the tongue among our members, that it defileth the whole body, and setteth on fire the course of nature; and it is set on fire of hell. For every kind of beasts, and of birds, and of serpents, and of things in the sea, is tamed, and hath been tamed of mankind: but the tongue can no man tame; it is an unruly evil, full of deadly poison." James is not talking to strangers. He is saying these things to each of us personally, just the way in which we are.

Another translation of what we have just read follows, "The human tongue is physically small, but what tremendous effects it can boast of! A whole forest can be set ablaze by a tiny spark of fire, and the tongue is as dangerous as any fire, with vast potentialities for evil. It can poison the whole body, it can make the whole of life a blazing hell. Beasts, birds, reptiles and all kinds of sea-creatures can be, and in fact are, tamed by man, but no one can tame the human tongue. It is an evil always liable to break out, and the poison it spreads is deadly" (James 3:5 - 8, *Phillips*).

Another translator phrased it this way, "So with the tongue. It is a small member but it can make huge claims. What a huge stack of timber can be set ablaze by the tiniest spark! And the tongue is in effect a fire. It represents among our members the world with all its wickedness; it pollutes our whole being; it keeps the wheel of our existence red-hot, and its flames are fed by hell. Beasts and birds of every kind, creatures that crawl on the ground or swim in the sea, can be subdued and have been subdued by mankind; but no man can subdue the tongue. It is an intractable evil, charged with deadly venom" (James 3:5 - 8, *New English Bible*). This version is based exactly on what we have here in our Bible. The translator is a Greek scholar as were the others. He expresses this passage the way he understands it in the Greek.

Another Greek scholar writes in still another way about the unruly nature of the tongue. As we read let us each one remember James is referring to us as we are. The tongue in itself is simply our inward ideas being formulated and being formed. Let us keep this in mind as we read: "This is how it is with the tongue: small as it is, it can boast about great things. Just think how large a forest can be set on fire by a tiny flame! And the tongue is like a fire. It is a world of wrong, occupying its place in our bodies and spreading evil through our whole being! It sets on fire the entire course of our existence with the fire which comes to it from hell itself. Man is able to tame, and has tamed, all other creatures — wild animals and birds, reptiles and fish. But no man has ever been able to tame the tongue. It is evil and uncontrollable, full of deadly poison" (James 3:5 - 8, *Today's English Version*).

James is actually emphasizing that all this applies to us. He is talking about the human nature of each of us. No wonder that in the days when we were unbelievers we had trouble controlling it. No wonder we had such trouble with ourselves. Only the grace of God can help us to deny ourselves.

Still another translation reads like this: "Even so the tongue is a little member, and it can boast of great things. See how much wood or how great a forest a tiny spark can set ablaze! And the tongue [is] a fire. [The tongue is a] world of wickedness set among our members, contaminating and depraving the whole body and setting on fire the wheel of birth — the cycle of man's nature — being itself ignited by hell (Gehenna). For every kind of beast and bird, of reptile and sea animal, can be tamed and has been tamed by human genius (nature). But the human tongue can be tamed by no man. It is (an undisciplined, irreconcilable) restless evil, full of death-bringing poison" (James 3:5 - 8, *Amplified*).

James helps us to see that the tongue, small as it is, expresses our mind, ourselves. All the perils of our human imagination, including covetousness, envy, jealousy, lusts and our private thoughts, run and rave like a forest fire. "The human heart is exceedingly sinful, wicked beyond belief." James dealing with our human nature, with ourselves as we are, warns us: "Watch it! You cannot control it!" Reading all this, we can only ask, what hope is there for us? The answer is, yield yourself to God. Deny the flesh. We must crucify the "natural man" in us. "Crucifying the flesh with the affections and lusts thereof."

These words are among the most clear-cut statements in the Bible. Here it is as plain as day that no amount of training will ever result in godliness. There is no possible way to discipline human nature into something acceptable to God. Thank God there is a way. The Bible way is, "Ye must be born again" (John 3:7).

Our natural heart is just like this tongue James is talking about. He shows how our thoughts will ordinarily run. For example, someone does something to us that we do not like and we go driving off in our car, or we go to work or to our place of business. We are annoyed and we think and think. And what are we thinking? When we are off by ourselves that way, how do our minds run? Generally speaking, our minds do not run to kind thoughts. Generally speaking, we are not thinking faithful or generous thoughts. Generally speaking, our thoughts are vain, envious and selfish. We must admit, we are just terrible. When we realize this, when we look into ourselves we know what we are, then we see what a wonderful thing the Gospel is. We can actually be saved from ourselves by the grace of God, which is in Christ. And we praise and worship Him.

Chapter 24

OUT OF THE SAME MOUTH

Therewith bless we God, even the Father; and therewith curse we men, which are made after the similitude of God. Out of the same mouth proceedeth blessing and cursing. My brethren, these things ought not so to be (James 3:9, 10).

A number of years ago I was interested in promoting a garden, and so I undertook to cultivate one. The first year I tried it I didn't get anything. The second year I tried it brought the same result, so I gave it up. I said the soil isn't any good. Then a young man came to the seminary where I was teaching. He asked me whether I was interested in having a garden. I said, "Yes, but this soil will not grow anything." We were standing on the grounds of the seminary, out beyond the buildings. He asked, "Where did you try to have it?" I pointed "over there." He said "What do you mean it won't grow anything? Look it's got weeds growing on it." I looked at him as he made this single comment with a smile: "Don't you know that any soil which will grow weeds will grow beans?"

I want to pass this on to you. Any of us who can walk in the wrong way, could walk in the right way. Any of us who walk in darkness, could walk in the light. Any of us who walk away from God, could walk to God. We will keep these thoughts in mind as we read along in the book of James. We have kept in mind that James is writing to Christians. He does not discuss how to become a Christian. He writes to people who already are Christians. He does not need to discuss with them what it means to be a Christian. They already know. James instead discusses how to live the Christian life. Speaking of the tongue, James says, "Therewith bless we God, the Father; and therewith we curse men." "Out of the same mouth" — just like a garden; out of the same soil we can have beans or weeds. Out of the same mouth we can have cursing or prayer.

It is a universal truth among all people, spiritually speaking, that impression must have expression to be healthy. If we feel inwardly moved, we must outwardly act, or we will suffer loss. We have seen how James takes the tongue as a case in point. He does not spell it out in so many words that he is talking about self-denial. However, as we read his words he makes it plain that if we let the tongue run wild this will be evil. He is referring to the inner thoughts of man, the kind of thinking we do inside our own selves where no one can stop us. James shows us that the tongue, our inner thinking apparatus, could be neutral but is often evil. Humanly speaking, naturally speaking it is evil, but it does not have to be so. It can be used for being godly. This is a graphic revelation of human nature. James wants us to realize that none of us can by himself tame the tongue, nor human nature, nor the flesh. All need the grace of God operative in our hearts.

This truth is very important for anyone interested in Christian education. When we think about the education of young people, of bringing children into a Christian experience, we should look closely at what James is setting forth. We cannot control human beings any more than we can control the tongue. There is an incorrigible aspect about mankind. It is simply idealistic talk to assume that it is possible to train man to do right and to do good. We wonder how knowledgeable such talkers are about this whole matter. How many of them realize what they are talking about? We might wonder whether they have children in their homes. If they do have children it would seem they would have ample evidence.

Where do people live who say that mankind is good? Do they live in a city? Do they live anywhere near people? Do they have any neighbors or relatives? If they do, how can they say people are good? What are they looking at when they say that people are just naturally good? The truth of the matter is that on every side there is evidence that as the tongue is an unruly member of our body, so is the whole nature of man. It is willful, self-inclined, self-indulgent, and proud, envious of other people and jealous of other people. All of these characteristics appear in mankind. "There is none that doeth good, no not one" (Romans 3:12).

James does not deal with solving the problems of mankind, since human nature is unreliable. Jesus Himself said about man, "But those things which proceed out of the mouth come forth from the heart; and they defile the man" (Matthew 15:18). James speaks of the tongue and here the Lord Jesus speaks of "out of the mouth" pointing out that the words we utter, the thoughts we entertain come first from the heart. "For out of the heart proceed evil thoughts, murders, adulteries, thefts, false witness, blasphemies" (Matthew 5:20). These are the things that defile a man, and they come from the inside. The Lord Jesus Christ went on to say that "to eat with unwashen hands defileth not a man" (Matthew 5:20). When a man's hands are dirty from working in the sand, or working in the mud, or working in the grease of the garage, the man is not really defiled.

It is the inward thoughts of a man coming through the mind, uttered by the tongue, that defile a man. This is what the tongue actually does. Now James is not pointing out these things because he has any hope that we will be able to control either ourselves or other people. He has already said that the tongue is an unruly member full of deadly poison. It is evil. Why is it evil? Because we are evil. Deep down in our hearts we are sinful.

Yet we must speak of these things in being faithful to the truth James is bringing to us. There is a reason why we talk about these things. There is a reason why preachers talk about them. Listen! James has the cure; preachers know the cure. The Lord Jesus Christ said, "Ye must be born again." This is it. Thank God this can happen. This is what we need to keep in mind at all times.

Now we come back to our first idea. If the ground can grow weeds, it can grow beans. The mouth that expresses profanity can also express blessing. A mouth that can be used in violent argument can also be used in gentle praise. If we can use our minds and thoughts to harm people, we could use our minds and thoughts to seek to benefit people. James is showing us that what we actually and truly need is a new birth.

Chapter 25

A GOOD TREE BRINGS GOOD FRUIT

> Doth a fountain send forth at the same place sweet water and bitter? Can the fig tree, my brethren, bear olive berries? either a vine, figs? so can no fountain both yield salt water and fresh. Who is a wise man and endued with knowledge among you? let him show out of a good conversation his works with meekness of wisdom (James 3:11 - 13).

James writes in a distinctive way all his own. But the thoughts he expresses are the thoughts of God. The Holy Spirit of God uses the mind of James as he writes his epistle. The Spirit of God speaks through him. We may speak of James as a particular person with a particular personality, but the truth of the matter is that he is being moved by the Holy Spirit of God to say the things he says.

James shows in his writing the concern that the Lord Jesus Christ Himself has that His members should be fruitful. The concern that the Lord has for fruitfulness in the life of a Christian is twofold. As the Gospel is presented to the Christian it has two aspects. One aspect is that of the Christian's inner experience. For instance, when we hear the Gospel and believe it, no one else knows that we believe it. No one on the outside knows that we have righteousness and joy and peace in the Holy Spirit. That is an inward, personal thing. Of course, it will have some outward manifestation in the course of time. But our personal acceptance of the promises of God in Christ Jesus happens inside our hearts.

There is another aspect of response: our testimony, our outward conduct as we witness to other people. When we are called to the Lord Jesus Christ and urged to put our trust in Him, the first thing that happens to us is that we will be forgiven. We will be redeemed and the whole operation of salvation will take place in us. We are saved! "Whosoever believeth in him shall not perish but have everlasting life" (John 3:16). This would happen if we were shut up in the dark for the rest of our days. If we were to be paralyzed at the moment that we believed in the Lord Jesus Christ, and could not move a muscle or utter a word, we would still be saved. We could still rejoice because Christ Jesus died for us. This is not because of anything we did, it is what the Lord does. Jehovah is our Saviour. The Lord Himself saves us, and He wants us to witness and testify to other people.

Oftentimes we are inclined to think that witnessing and testifying is a matter of saying words. It is true that words may be included as part of our witness and testimony. However, the Apostle Paul writes, "Ye know what manner of men we were among you, for your sakes." It is in our living relations with others that we actually do this witnessing.

It is in our relations with others that we face the issue of self. As surely as we walk with the Lord we will have to deal with ourselves. This inward reality of self is a good deal like the constant pull of gravity on anything, that gives weight to an object. That weight is the pull of gravity that pulls the ball down to earth. We are able to lift the ball because our arm is stronger than the pull downward. Because we can move the ball, we can handle the ball anyway we want to. This does not stop the pull of gravity but it overcomes it. That is the way it is with a Christian. We have this situation in ourselves. We have it in our human nature and that human nature is constant. It will pull us down with our own weight. It will always pull us down into the things that are natural. But the power of the Spirit of God in Christ Jesus sets us free from these things. By yielding ourselves to Him, we will be lifted above our natural selves.

Now these are the things that James is concerned about. He is concerned that we should be lifted above the natural to the point where the effect of the grace of God could be seen. Our witness, our outward conduct, our personal testimony among people is seen in our inter-personal relationships — the way we deal with people. James is concerned about what is involved in inconsistent behavior. This is what troubles him. The very fact that he discusses inconsistent behavior with the brethren shows that this is a constant problem. It can happen to anyone of us, that our natural self may lead us away from the will of God.

Taking an illustration from the natural world James writes, "Doth a fountain send forth at the same place sweet water and bitter?" Just as this is true in natural things, it is true with a Christian. Anyone would know this. We just do not expect to have good water and bad water coming out of the same fount. Carrying on the same emphasis James continues, "Can the fig tree, my brethren, bear olive berries? either a vine, figs? so can no fountain both yield salt water and fresh." This is a practical line of thought. We do not need unusual insight to follow what James has to say. But there is an unusual application being made here.

How would this truth be seen in our lives as Christians? Have we ever been in a Sunday school class where instead of studying the lesson of the day, all the time was spent in discussing a football game of the day before? Is that the thing to do? Is that what the students are to expect? It is as if we turned on the fountain to get fresh water and salt water came out. James is saying that this does not make sense. Have we ever gone to the Men's Bible Class on Sunday morning and found that instead of the Bible study we expected, the time was given over to discussing politics? This could be especially so, in a presidential election year. James would say, this does not make sense. This sort of thing leaves a bad impression. James is concerned about the effect we have on other people.

"Who is a wise man and endued with knowledge among you? let him show out of a good conversation his works with meekness of wisdom." We notice that James has not said anything about virtue. He hasn't said anything about being good. He has not said anything about being pious, about being spiritual. He talks about having good sense. "Who is a wise man": who is a person with good common sense "and endued with knowledge?" Who has sense enough to come in when it rains? Where is there such a person? "Good conversation" means, good manner of life.

Christians dealing with other people should show "his works with meekness of wisdom." He can be wise and he can have knowledge but he must never be over-bearing. He cannot be proud, but he must quietly and meekly act with good sense. This is what James is trying to tell us. He is saying that if we do just that, our outward testimony among other people will be good and it will be effective.

Chapter 26

AN EARTHLY MIND IS EVIL

But if ye have bitter envying and strife in your hearts, glory not, and lie not against the truth. This wisdom decendeth not from above, but is earthly, sensual, devilish. For where envying and strife is, there is confusion and every evil work (James 3:14-16).

It is not hard to understand that bitterness, contention and quarrelling are evil. But it is rather hard to remember that James is writing to Christians to draw their attention to something they need to hear. There can be in believers that which is still natural and human. This would be from the earth, earthy, as it were, and in itself evil.

The Bible speaks of earthly things and of heavenly things. The Apostle Paul referring to these speaks of flesh and spirit, as we might speak of something as being carnal or spiritual. This refers to two spheres of living, two separate areas. When we speak of the flesh, that refers to the human, the natural. Every human being has a natural human nature. James calls it earthly. This nature operates by sense, by the way we feel, by the way we hear and see and smell and taste and touch. The other sphere is in the spirit. This is spiritual and is called heavenly, and it operates by faith.

The natural or the earthly sphere centers in the ego, the I. As a human being I become conscious of me, myself, I. This is natural to man. The second sphere or area, called the heavenly, centers in Christ. We are members of His Body. He is the Head. This is not natural to man. This is something that God does. The first, which is natural, raises the question: "What will I do?

What must I do?" The second, which is spiritual, raises the question, "What would God do? What will Christ Jesus do in me?" Paul contrasts the origin of these two spheres by saying, "the natural, the earthly, comes from beneath, whereas the heavenly comes from above."

Both earthly and heavenly natures are operative in the believer. The things of Christ which are set forth in the Bible come into the heart, like rain comes upon the soil from above. The things of the flesh, the things of the natural human being, come from beneath. They come from .the nature of man. A Christian may yet have a carnal mind with earthy thoughts. James is concerned that no Christian having such natural, carnal, earthy thoughts should deceive himself. They are really a part of his old human nature and come from the flesh. If you have such thoughts don't fool yourself into thinking that you do not have anything wrong with you.

James is saying, because you are a Christian does not mean that everything is all right. Being a Christian will save your soul, that's true. Being a Christian and trusting in the Lord Jesus Christ will reconcile you to the Father, that's true! But the old man in you, the flesh in you, needs to be denied. If you have bitter envying and strife in your heart, if you dislike people and are against them, "glory not" — don't fool yourself and "lie not against the truth." Do not ignore such feelings and do not deny them. As sure as you have envying and strife in your heart, you're carnal, brother. You have a carnal element in you that needs to be denied.

James goes on to say, "This wisdom cometh not from above, but is earthly, sensual, devilish." "Earthly" means that it is of the flesh, out of the physical being. It is generated in the consciousness of the ego — it is natural and it is in everyone. "Sensual" refers to feelings and emotions and desires. It could be called psychological. These things need not be ugly in themselves. They can be refined and artistic, but they will always have some aspects of pleasing and lifting oneself. When James writes about something being devilish he does not mean that it is like the devil, but rather that is originates from the devil. How would something originate from the devil? We need only remember the thing he did in the Garden of Eden. Satan will take some one thing that appeals to us and draw our attention to it until we desire it. When we act according to our desire, our actions may be all wrong. We keep thinking about this one thing we want until we will even disobey God to obtain it.

This is what happened to Judas. He thought of one thing: money. He kept thinking and thinking about money, and the first thing he knew he betrayed his Lord for money. Afterward when he saw what he had done he went and hanged himself, but that was beside the point. He was thinking of just one thing when the time came to act. Such a frame of mind is of the devil. So it can be with any of us. If we think of only one thing and desire it, we can be tempted to go in the wrong direction. If I think of only one thing and set my heart on it, I can make a big mistake and sin against God.

James continues his discussion, "For where envying and strife is, there is confusion and every evil work." Where there is envying and strife, destructive attitudes toward other people follow. We do not want them to have what they have. We wish we had what they have and we will fight with them about what they have. This causes confusion and is ungodly. Why does it cause confusion? Because the flesh that is in us will lead us away from God and the grace that is in us will lead us toward the Lord. So we are torn between wanting to do His will and turning away from His will. We turn to God and we are pulled away from Him. It is a confusing thing when we want to keep our cake and eat it, too. That's confusion! If we want to save our money and have a bank account, that's one thing. If we want to spend it, that's another. Now if we want both to save it and spend it, we are in confusion. If we want both, to work and to play, there is confusion. If we as Christians act according to the flesh which will be earthly and sinful, while our hearts want to please God in obedience, we will be thrown into confusion. May the Lord help us to yield ourselves entirely to Him that we may know the blessing of God which comes when we receive wisdom from above.

Chapter 27

WISDOM FROM ABOVE IS PURE

> But the wisdom that is from above is first pure, then peaceable, gentle, and easy to be entreated, full of mercy and good fruits, without partiality, and without hypocrisy. And the fruit of righteousness is sown in peace of them that make peace (James 3:17, 18).

How often we have longed for a frame of mind where every thought would be kind, godly and peaceful. James tells us that such thoughts do not come from within. Perhaps no one will ever have such a mind completely, nor continuously, so that every day is exactly alike, and yet Christians can have such thoughts and such moments. Although these thoughts do not come from within, they appear within. They are in our hearts and minds when we become conscious of them. Now we could not make a bigger mistake than to assume that we ourselves thought of them. No: godly, kind, peaceful thoughts come from above.

The appearance of such thoughts remind us of an artesian well. When we see such a well with a stream of water pouring out, we can be sure there is a source of that water higher up. It is only when water gathers in some place up on the mountains and then comes down underground where we live that we can dig down and tap it. If conditions are right we can actually have water flowing out of such a well like a spring.

It is this way when one becomes a Christian. The Lord Jesus Christ speaking of believers said that out of their inward parts will flow rivers of living water. This is true of all Christians.

This can be true of us when we believe in Christ. We do not produce such godliness. It does not originate within us. This is something God does for us. He works in our hearts that which is well pleasing in His sight.

When James uses the word "wisdom" he means "frame of mind." This wisdom he speaks of, this frame of mind, these thoughts that we have in our consciousness, these ideas we hold in our awareness which are so gracious, come from above. Like the waters of an artesian well, they come up in our hearts. Actually they come from above into our hearts by the grace of God. James comments, ". . . this wisdom that is from above is first pure." When we see the word "pure" in the New Testament we can substitute the word "unselfish." Our thoughts are "pure" when there is nothing about self in them.

When we have selfishness, pride and vanity, our consciousness of self is to be seen. Then we are manifesting something that will ruin what is from God. The wisdom that is from above is first pure (no idea of self in connection with it) and then "peaceable" — meaning peace-loving, peaceful, living at peace with the neighbors. "Peaceable, gentle, and easy to be entreated" — these are agreeable persons because they easily forgive. They are ready to be gracious: "easy to be entreated, full of mercy and good fruits." "Full of mercy and good fruits" — they are ready at all times to show mercy. If someone needed mercy they would gladly show it. They would have it in their hearts and minds to be kind to others. They would want to be helpful. "Full of mercy and good fruits, without partiality" — showing no favoritism. With one person just as good as another, they will see them exactly alike without hypocrisy: no subterfuge, nothing hidden in any way.

The "fruit of righteousness" does not refer to something righteousness produces. When we say "the fruit of righteousness" we mean righteousness itself is the fruit. When we say it "is sown in peace" we mean to say that the people who produce righteousness are the kind of people who in themselves have peace.

As an illustration of a person who was making peace, let us remember the occasion when Abraham and Lot came to the point of separation. Abraham suggested to Lot that he should choose whichever section of the country he wanted. Abraham told Lot, "It is not a good thing for our servants to fight. It does not set a good example. Others will get the wrong impression of us. So in order that our servants will not fight we should separate. There should be no fighting over property. Look out over the whole countryside and take what you want, and I'll take what is left" (Genesis 13:5 - 9, paraphrased).

Lot chose the plains that led down into Sodom and Gomorrah, which was a rich and fertile country. Abraham went the opposite way up into the mountains. He found a plain up there, the plain of Mamre. Here he built himself an altar, where he could worship God. In this fashion Abraham made peace in a very simple way: he simply gave Lot his choice.

This could be seen if two boys came into a room wanting to sit down where there was just one chair. Normally there would be struggling and tussling, perhaps a real pulling match. Each boy would want to grab the chair. Each one would want to hang on to it. How could this fussing and pulling and quarrelling be stopped? This could be done very simply: let one of the boys give the chair to the other one. There would be no more quarrelling, no more fighting over the chair. The boy who gave up the chair to let the other boy have it would be the peacemaker. He made peace by giving up his claim.

This kind of peace making is actually righteousness before God. Seeking the will of God first and looking to Him would certainly keep us from quarrelling with a fellow believer over something we wanted for ourselves. In this way we will secure righteousness. It would be "sown in peace of them that make peace." When we promote that kind of peace, we do not do it because we have to. "To sow in peace" means without contention, without strife. This "sowing" is done quietly and peaceably and God will bless it with more and more peace.

We read in the Bible, "A soft answer turneth away wrath" (Proverbs 15:1). This also enters into the picture. If we really want to be peaceful and quiet, we will want to be gentle and full of mercy. If we are not peace-makers we cannot be like that. We cannot be like that if we fuss and fight. When James says, "The fruit of righteousness will be sown in peace of them that make peace," he is showing to us that it is possible to have a godly frame of mind. It is possible to think in terms of getting along with other people and meaning them well. This attitude of mind comes from above. This is from God.

Chapter 28

ORIGIN OF WAR

From whence come wars and fightings among you? come they
not hence, even of your lusts that war in your members? Ye
lust, and have not: ye kill, and desire to have, and cannot obtain (James 4:1, 2a).

There is an underlying cause of strife and contention and war.
The full answer to war may become involved, but the basic
principles involved may easily be recognized. James deals with
this matter very concisely and gives a real explanation for the
source of strife and fighting. James is not discussing war among
mankind as a whole. He is not particularly thinking about war
as a social disorder. He is thinking about quarrelling and feud-
ing and strife among believers who could be doing better in
living.

No doubt there is war going on all over the world. War among
all men stems from the same root as war among Christians. Although no restraint is seen among men in the world, there should
be restraint among Christians. James is disturbed when he sees
contention, strife and quarrelling occurring among them. He is
deeply moved and concerned when Christians quarrel and feud
with each other. So James raises the question, why? In his reply
he brings out very simply, very plainly: they are not completely
yielded to God. He says this to believers, to Christians.

Another translation of these verses reads like this, "What leads
to strife, to discord and feud? How do conflicts, quarrels and
fightings originate among you? Do they not arise from your
sensual desires, that are ever warring in your bodily members?
You are jealous and covet, and your desires go unfulfilled so that

119

you become murderers. You burn with envy and anger, not able to obtain the contentment and the happiness that you seek. So you fight and war."

When he uses the expression, ". . . sensual desires that are warring in your members," James is referring to the fact that in ourselves we Christians have interests and desires that conflict because they are opposed to each other. We may, for instance, have the desire to use a certain amount of money for ourselves; we'd like to eat something, we'd like to drink something, to do something to make us feel real good. At the same time we see someone who is in need and we would like to give him some money. We would like to give him something, so that he would be able to go on about his work and feel better. Obviously we can't do both. If we spend it, we can't give it. If we give it, we can't use it. This causes confusion in ourselves, in our own members.

We find in ourselves such conflicting desires: we'd like to go and help people in need, and we'd like to drive on down the road and mind our own business. So there is contention going on in us. James expresses it by saying, ". . . you desire and you have not. You kill and you cannot obtain your desire." The particular translation we have just read states in this way, "You are jealous and covet [what others have] and your desires go unfulfilled; [so] you become murderers. . . . You burn with envy and anger and are not able to obtain [the gratification, the contentment and the happiness you seek], so you fight and war." (James 4:2a, *Amplified*).

Let us look at another translation of this same passage. "Where do all the fights and quarrels among you come from?" (James 4:1, *Today's English Version*). He is asking the question of Christians. Someone may say, 'Well, I don't think that a real Christian will be like this." It probably is true that a mature Christian who is entirely yielded to the Lord would not do this sort of thing. Unfortunately, not all Christians are full grown. "Where do quarrels among you come from? They come from your passions. You Christians are constantly fighting within your own bodies. You want things, but cannot have them, so you quarrel and fight." This is truly the way that Christian people actually get into quarrelling with each other. Deep down in themselves they are quarrelling with themselves. They are ready to kill because they want things and cannot have them.

Another translation of this same portion of Scripture reads thus: "What causes conflict and quarrels among you? Do they not spring from the aggressiveness of your bodily desires? You want something which you cannot have, and so you are bent on murder; you are envious, and cannot attain your ambition, so you quarrel and fight" (James 4:1, 2, *New English Bible*).

Still another translation reads like this: "But what about the feuds and struggles that exist among you . . . ? Can't you see that they arise from conflicting passions within yourselves? You crave for something and don't get it; you are murderously jealous of what others have got and which you can't possess yourselves; you struggle and fight with one another" (James 4:1, 2, *Phillips*). This is actually the way James is accounting for the fact that Christian people get into a quarrelsome relationship with other people. It is simply because they want things they cannot obtain.

At this point we should remember what the Apostle Paul has to say along this line. Paul would explain to us that there is a way in which we could get over this fighting and striving and be free from it. This change would come only from self denial. If we really deny ourselves, and reckon ourselves dead, if we retire from the race, all would be changed. If we surrender and give up our ambitions to grasp and to have, there would not be this fussing, this quarrelling, and this anger and frustration. This is the way in which James has pointed out to us the origin of strife and contention.

Chapter 29

BARREN PRAYING

. . . ye fight and war, yet ye have not, because ye ask not. Ye ask, and receive not, because ye ask amiss, that ye may consume it upon your lusts (James 4:2b, 3).

In his comments about praying James does not analyze Christian experience, he just describes it. When Paul wrote about the life of a Christian, he explained about flesh and spirit. James simply refers to that which comes from beneath, which is flesh; and that which comes from above, which is spirit. Both of these writers recognize that a Christian has two natures operative in him. All through the New Testament it is recognized that believers have both flesh and spirit, because they have both a body and a soul. The flesh is human nature. In the soul a man can be born again and have his spiritual nature there. These two natures are operative in the Christian in varying degrees, not to the same extent in everyone, nor at all times.

In discussing this problem of praying James sets forth his ideas in plain language. He uses sharp words as he exposes the truth about praying, as when he says, "Ye fight and war, yet ye have not, because ye ask not." How often Christians struggle and strive with each other for the same things. They quarrel with each other, as to which one should be first or as to which one should have a particular honor. They contend with each other, pulling and pushing so far as they're concerned, because of what they strive for — and yet they do not achieve it. "Ye have not." All of the contention is to no end. How often we hear of such quarrels taking place to no purpose. None of them really matter. All this happens "because ye ask not."

James is saying to Christians that all this striving, this contending, this fighting and fussing can't get them anywhere because they do not turn to God for help. The whole Christian point of view is based on a simple idea, a simple promise: we cannot do anything in ourselves. No human being can live out the full significance of life in his own human strength. We need help, God's help.

In discussing the lack of results James explains, "Ye ask, and receive not, because ye ask amiss, that ye may consume it upon your lusts." We must be careful in regard to the meaning of this word "lust" in the New Testament. It does not necessarily mean anything vicious or crude or vulgar. Of course it is sinful and it is evil, but it could be refined, it could be perfumed, it could be sophisticated, it could be educated, and it could be civilized. We could have very dainty desires, but if we follow through on them, no matter how delicate, that would be just as sinful as if they were crude and violent and vulgar. "Ye ask, and ye receive not." We can actually go through the motions and say the words, but we will not get any answer, because we went about it in the wrong way. "Ye ask amiss that ye may consume it upon your lusts." We ask just for what we wanted for ourselves. How often this would describe praying in general.

We might ask, "Why should we pray? Don't we pray to get things?" In the same way we might ask, "Why should we work?" Do we not work to get things? James does not spell out the answers to these questions for us, but we can see the truth that is here for us. The common, universal way of doing things is that we go out and work for ourselves. This is what everyone would think. This is the natural way of doing things, the human way of doing things. But it is not the Christian way of doing things. The Lord Jesus Christ said, "If any man will come after me, let him deny himself" (Matthew 16:24). Now if we deny ourselves, and reckon ourselves dead, we no longer have the same kind of interests. As Christians we have the mind of Christ Jesus in us, and not our own. Do we remember His words? "I do nothing of myself, I do all things to please my Father" (paraphrase). If His mind is in us He will move us to do all things that would please Almighty God rather than for any personal benefits as the results of our efforts.

What should parents be thinking about when they plan to do

something for their children? Should they be thinking only about the child, or should they think about the child under God? Do they want the blessing upon that child as God would have it, or do they want the blessing upon their child for the child's sake alone? If they have in mind having blessing upon the child just for the child's sake, they are going to be disappointed. How many parents have found that true. They have done so much, suffered so much, sacrificed so much for the child alone, and the child is growing up to be utterly selfish, entirely independent of the parents. As a result the parents mourn all through the years, languishing, in a sense of disappointment, frustration and defeat because the child has grown up intent only on himself. Yet this is exactly what they trained the child to be!

It was not good enough when the parents made their plans for the child and thought only to benefit the child or themselves. Christians must do all things as unto God. They must accept the child as from God. God's will in the life of the child is far more important than the child's pleasure. Only when they ask things for the child for the glory of God, can they be sure that their prayers for him will be answered.

This same thing would apply in our own lives as Christians. We could pray, as to whether we should live or die, whether we'll be rich or poor, whether we will be sick or well in the course of life, but if we pray all this in order that we may prosper, that we may better ourselves, James would say, "Ye ask amiss." If, instead, we had in mind that we wanted to serve God, that we wanted to be with God, His will would be our will. If being in God's will would mean that we were going to be sick or lose a leg or die, His will for us would be right. Being in His will is more important than health or life. In our work and in our prayers we can confidently expect blessing if we seek to glorify God in all we do. Why should we do these things? That we might live in His presence, in communion with Him, pleasing Him. Then the Spirit of our Lord Jesus Christ will be seen in us, who did all things to please His Father.

Chapter 30

FRIENDSHIP WITH THE WORLD

Ye adulterers and adulteresses, know ye not that the friendship
of the world is enmity with God? whosoever therefore will be a
friend of the world is the enemy of God (James 4:4).

I John 2:15 - 17 gives a good definition of what the Bible
means by "world." "Love not the world, neither the things that
are in the world. If any man love the world, the love of the
Father is not in him. For all that is in the world, the lust of the
flesh, and the lust of the eyes, and the pride of life, is not of the
Father, but is of the world. And the world passeth away, and the
lust thereof: but he that doeth the will of God abideth for ever."
The word "world" in the Bible refers to anything that appeals to
appetite, to imagination and pride. Our whole manner of thinking, our whole frame of mind, if we are being stirred by what
we want to further our own imagination and vanity and appetites,
would actually be termed "of the world."

James has a pointed word about this. He has something to
say to all Christians in James 4:4. This verse seems to be ignored
by many who read the Bible. Seemingly it has never really attracted attention. How many believers go along blindly as though
this verse had never been written? Let us read it again for emphasis and to catch its full meaning: "Ye adulterers and adulteresses, know ye not that the friendship of the world is enmity
with God? whosoever therefore will be a friend of the world is
the enemy of God." That's pretty plain! That's straight-out talk!

When James uses the designations, "adulterers and adulteresses," he is not referring particularly to physical adultery. This
is not so much a matter of sexual disorder and sin. It is referring

to something of the Spirit — something of the heart. This refers to divided love and affection. These words show the Old Testament influence in James' mind. Out of all the New Testament writers James is most impressed by the writings of the prophets, particularly of the minor prophets. One of these prophets proclaimed that Israel was a chosen Bride as far as God was concerned. Israel was to have as close a relationship with God as that which exists between husband and wife. When Israel became interested in worshiping other false gods, when their hearts which were committed to God turned to idols, the prophets called it adultery.

Basically that's what adultery is. That is what we have here: the interest in the things of this world actually dividing the basic interest of our hearts. We must realize that when we accept Christ as our Saviour we form a kind of relationship that calls for complete committal. As in marriage vows, calling for the forsaking of all others, so it should be spiritually speaking. When we put God first and above everything else, then our relationship is right and proper.

The Apostle Paul speaks of the church as the Bride, and John the Baptist spoke of the Lord Jesus Christ as the Bridegroom. This is the relationship which exists between the Church and the Lord Jesus Christ. This is the relationship which exists between each believer and the Lord. Whatever we love is the object of our esteem; what we love most, we esteem higher than anything else, we adore more than anything else. Whatever we put first in our life above everything else is what we love.

The first commandment says, "Thou shalt love the Lord thy God and Him only shalt thou serve" (paraphrase). The Lord God Himself later said, "If ye love me, keep my commandments" (John 14:15). In other words, keeping the commandments of God, doing the will of God, being obedient to His will, comes above everything else. This must come first. It came first with our Lord Jesus Christ, who said, "I do always the things that please my Father." On another occasion He said, "My Father worketh hitherto, and I work." "The Son can do nothing of himself" (John 5:17, 19). The Apostle Paul tells us about people "who were lovers of pleasure more than lovers of God." At another time Paul wrote, "Demas hath forsaken me, having loved this present world" (II Timothy 4:10). The love Demas had for the world misled him. James tells us "that the friendship of the world is enmity with God."

Have we ever wondered about this phrase in the Old Testament, "I the Lord thy God am a jealous God" (Exodus 20:5)? If we have ever considered this an unfortunate translation, we would have been so wrong. When there is love involved, then jealousy is proper. When is jealousy a part of virtue and godliness? When we are jealous about that which belongs to us in love. When the husband is jealous of his wife's affections and the wife is jealous of her husband's devotion, these things are proper. True love has an exclusiveness about it. There is an intolerance in true love. This is not friendship, this is love. This is the kind of relationship wherein one commits one's self to the other. When a wife commits herself to her husband, it is this one and no other. Forsaking all others she turns his way. That is the way it is in the marriage vows, and that is the way it is spiritually speaking. When we put God first and above everything else, when He is in our hearts, we have nothing left to love anyone else. If we really love God and turn our hearts to Him, we don't want to love anyone else. That is why "to be a friend of the world, is to be an enemy of God."

This is a sobering line of thought, as we go over it again in our minds. "Know ye not that the friendship of the world is enmity with God?" This does not mean that when we are friendly with people, that's contrary to God. That's not the point. It is when we give room in our hearts for the things of appetite and imagination, the things that make for vanity and pride, that we become "lovers of pleasure more than lovers of God." God knows this. God feels this!

God will take second place to no one and nothing. No! God is first. He is above all. There is an integrity about this, that is proper. All this James stresses in the sense we have discussed. He has brought out the fact that we are so often inclined to be influenced by our natural desires, our own human natures: and our own human nature will lead us astray. If we go by the things that lead to pride and vanity, if we indulge our appetites and imagination, we will actually be enemies of God.

Chapter 31

HE GIVETH MORE GRACE

> Do ye think that the scripture saith in vain, The spirit that dwelleth in us lusteth to envy? But he giveth more grace. Wherefore he saith,
> God resisteth the proud,
> but giveth grace unto the humble (James 4:5-6).

There is one way to escape from being involved in the struggle of seeking personal gain or advantage. This is made possible only by the grace of God.

"Do ye think that the scripture saith in vain, The spirit that dwelleth in us lusteth to envy?" This refers to what the Word of God has to say about the nature of man in himself, the human being. The Scriptures tell us that the nature of a man in himself is to want to advance himself. Man has a strong desire to try to get ahead of other people. The Bible reveals man with an inward drive to compete with other people, in the course of which he begins to envy other people. The word "lusteth" means that the spirit of man has a strong desire to lift himself beyond other people. In other words, "rivalry" becomes involved: trying to beat the other man in a race is just natural to mankind.

How old is a baby before he notices something he wants? How much older would he have to be before he notices and wants the bigger, brighter, more interesting things? We have all observed little children as they have an opportunity of getting something they think is better than what they already have. They'll throw away what they have and reach for the other. Just the other day I happened to be in a restaurant and saw something I don't think I'll ever forget. A father and a mother were sitting at a table eating. With them was a little child. I don't know how old this child was, but he looked to be about two years old. He could hardly talk, except for a few words, but I could hear him saying very plainly, "That's mine." This attracted my attention and I found that the baby said, "That's mine," about everything he saw. When I heard that little child cry out in a loud voice, "That's mine" to everything in sight, I thought, *How human.* What an ordinary human being this child is!

By the way, if you have ever noticed four or five boys crossing a lot, you will remember that they started to run, even when they didn't want to run. Why? One boy would start running and another would say, "Hey, don't run." But when the others started running he ran too. He couldn't help it. It's this inward drive. We see it on the playground and we'll see it in the house in the hall. If we have two little girls walking down the hall, first thing we know they are running. Trying to beat the other person to the end of the hall is just as natural as breathing.

We have noticed children coming home from school with their report cards. They compare each other's cards. The child with a good report card shows hers with pride. The one with the poor report card is hiding hers from the rest. Even as children we are so conscious of what others have and do. This situation does not stop with babies and children and students. How about a woman and her clothes? What is her attitude toward other people? Does she compare the appearance of her clothes to those worn by other women? I have known of a woman to leave a party because she saw another woman wearing a dress identical to her own. She simply could not stand it. It seemed to be a reflection on herself. Each of these cases was motivated by the same feeling of rivalry.

A man might not act that way about his suit, but how would he act about his car? How do men compare each other so far as their cars are concerned? Speaking of cars we need only get in the traffic on the freeway to notice how people will try to get ahead of one another. This is done for no particular reason. It is just human nature.

Even in churches much comparing goes on. Church members make comparisons as to the most beautiful chimes, the best organ, the most colorful windows, the nicest pews and the finest carpets! They compare themselves with other churches as to their choirs. Even preachers compare their sermons with those preached by other preachers. Where will this stop? It will not stop as long as there are human beings. It is characteristic of human beings to desire to rival others and to envy what others have.

This creates a universal problem. It is common to Christians because they inherit this problem from their human natures. They are quite helpless in the face of this urge to compare themselves with other people and to try to get ahead of them. In this hopeless situation the Gospel alone speaks of hope. "But He giveth more grace."

Grace is something God puts into our hearts, that enables us to do His will. For the Christians this is the grace of the Lord Jesus Christ, which is given to them. When Jesus Christ was here on earth He did the will of His Father. The grace that moved Christ Jesus into doing the will of His Father is now available for every Christian. "More grace?" Why more grace? More than we need! Ample for every situation. Despite the natural tendency on our part to covet, to try to get ahead, to be in front, the ample grace of God can deliver us from this natural urge.

Oh, what a wonderful thing it is, to realize from the bottom of our heart that we just don't care! If Tom gets ahead of us, and Dick gets ahead of us, and Harry gets ahead of us, what difference does it make? There is room for us, too. To experience this freedom we will need the grace of God in our hearts. And God giveth more grace. "God resisteth the proud, but He giveth grace to the humble." May God grant to everyone of us this wonderful blessing of more grace.

Chapter 32

DRAW NIGH TO GOD

Submit yourselves therefore to God. Resist the devil, and he will flee from you. Draw nigh to God, and he will draw nigh to you (James 4:7, 8a).

Many people like to read the book of James because the sentences are short, his ideas are clear, and he is talking straight. James is very realistic. He moves from point to point in a way that leaves no doubt as to where he is going. In James 4:7, 8a we are reminded again that these words could be addressed only to Christians. To understand them one must believe in God. For another thing one must recognize that there is a devil. Most important of all a Christian must keep in mind that he can do something about it. He can actually turn to God and resist the devil.

When we say that James writes to Christians, we wish that everyone were a Christian. There is no attempt to shut anyone out. The thing for us to realize is that James is too practical to think that he is telling the whole world what to do. His words wouldn't make sense to unbelievers. James is facing the facts of life realistically.

The facts of living are pretty much the same for a Christian as they are for a sailor as he sails the ocean. When a sailor sails the ocean in his ship he is constantly in danger. He is floating on top of his possible grave, every hour of the day, minute by minute. The ocean could drown him at any time. It's right there. This is certainly true in regard to a sailor. Can we realize that everyone of us is at all times in the presence of potential disaster? Something could happen to anyone of us at any time, just as it could to the man in the boat. We are sailing on an ocean that could drown us. This is the only way to understand life.

Jesus has made it clear that the natural man in himself is hopelessly in sin. He is in bondage to his inner spirit. Since sin has entered in, that is the way man is built. Man is a sinful being, and so is naturally selfish. We recognize that this is true. We may wish it were different but if we are honest we must admit it is true. Now, just as surely as our selfish, sinful way is true, there is something else that is also true: God is able to save! God can deliver!

We all face these two factors in life. It is true that we are in danger. We can shut our eyes like an ostrich and say that because we do not see it the danger is not there. But it is there and it is real. The second fact is, God is available. In Him is safety from all danger. When we say this, we are talking like Christians. We are expressing the way it is in a Christian's heart and mind. Certainly our bodies are in constant danger. And just as certainly our souls are constantly safe in the hand of God. Certainly things could happen to us that hurt, and just as certainly, God can keep us in any situation. So what should an intelligent person do, inasmuch as these two aspects are true?

In view of the fact that we are by nature not good, and that God in His power is gracious, what should we do? Come to God! James tells us to come to God because this is wisdom! He's not telling us what to do because he's an angel or especially good. He is telling us He wants us to use good sense. "Submit yourselves therefore to God." Yield yourselves therefore to God. Why "therefore"? In view of the peril in yourself, and in view of the help in God. You haven't got it, God has. God can! Under these circumstances, act with good sense. Exercise common sense: come to God.

Since we do not have what it takes within us, let us not trust in ourselves. "Submit yourselves therefore to God." What does this word "submit" mean? Yield yourself. Give in to God. Yielding would include that we accept the situation that we are in. For instance we live in a certain home. We have people living in it that have their peculiarities. All right! They had them yesterday and the day before. It's no secret that they are going to have them tomorrow. They are going to have them the day after.

People are that way. So we get used to it. As far as we are concerned let us accept our situation. I could say: "I think that's terrible." This may be true but something else is true, too. God is available to me. When I understand that the situation in my home and in my job is mine in His providence, I can accept it. If it is hard to bear I can ask for help to bear it. I can turn my thoughts to something else. When I realize that God in His providence had placed me in this situation I should not fuss about it, should not kick against it.

We may have some neighbors who are a real burden to bear. God knows about that. We may have hard things happen to us. God knows about that. When we submit ourselves to God, when we think about God, when we talk about the mercy of God, we will not think about circumstances, people or events. We will then remember Him, and in our hearts and minds we will pray to Him.

When we read the words, "Resist the devil, and he will flee from you," we may wonder how in the world we can resist him. The answer is, "Get on your knees." Here is a little line on this subject, and it's a good one. "Satan trembles when he sees, the weakest saint upon his knees." We can pick that up and walk with it. We can take it with us throughout the day. Let us not look at circumstances. Let us not ignore other people nor look down on other people. Let us look up to God. Let us pray. Let us read our Bibles. Even if we do not understand all of it, or know all that is in it. "Draw nigh to God, and he will draw nigh to you."

Reading our Bibles will bring us close to God. Going to church to worship God will bring us close to Him. When we ask others to come to church with us, when we share what we believe with someone else, we will be brought closer to God. Witnessing in telling others about the Lord will bring us close to God. It is wonderfully true that as believers draw nigh unto God, He will draw nigh unto everyone that believes. It is just as simple as that. There is safety from all danger when we are close to God.

CLEANSE FOR BLESSING

Cleanse your hands, ye sinners; and purify your hearts, ye double-minded. Be afflicted, and mourn, and weep: let your laughter be turned to mourning, and your joy to heaviness. Humble yourselves in the sight of the Lord, and he shall lift you up (James 4:8b-10).

When we say that we are believers we mean that we understand that God sent Jesus Christ into this world for us. We accept as a fact that He came into this world, suffered and died on our behalf, that we might be forgiven. There are people who feel that they do not need this. There are some to whom this action by God does not appeal. However, some day all must stand face to face with Him: the Judge of all men. They will then be judged by Almighty God, who is their Creator, and who is now offering them a way of escape by believing His Word.

We live in a world that has the Bible in it. Even if people do not read it, the Bible is still here. God put it here for a purpose. When we are all through, so far as this world is concerned, we will be called to stand in the presence of God. Would it surprise us if we were simply asked, What did you do with the Book? What did you do with the Bible? Did you look into it? Did you seek to understand the message of the Gospel?

Generally speaking, men expect Christians to be good. Men expect the Bible to tell the good person what he should do, and how he should do it. This sounds right, but the truth of living actually requires a more realistic view.

No man is good, nor can be become good by his own efforts. As far as a Christian is concerned, we can say right here and now, that if he believes in the Lord Jesus Christ this is good in itself. "What shall we do, that we might work the works of God? . . . This is the work of God, that ye believe on him, whom he hath sent" (John 6:28, 29). So every believer is good in the sight of God, when he believes in Him and obediently serves Him. The Christian's conduct resulting from his believing will really be the fruit of the Holy Spirit of God. Whatever is good in his conduct will thus be the work of God.

It may seem strange that James should write to Christians as if they were sinners, but in Chapter 4:8b - 10 we read words addressed to the wrongdoers. "Cleanse your hands, ye sinners." Sinners among Christians, sinners among believers. "Purify your hearts, ye double-minded." Christians who haven't got things straight. "Be afflicted, and mourn, and weep: let your laughter be turned to mourning, and your joy to heaviness" (James is saying — just be honest about this thing. You're in a bad way. You have been doing wrong, you're not well off). "Humble yourselves in the sight of the Lord, and he shall lift you up." Now in the old times a preacher preaching that would say, "Get right with God." Sometimes one of these old time preachers would speak even plainer. He would say, "Quit your meanness." They were telling the truth. This is exactly what James spells out to believers, to Christians. When we believe on the Lord Jesus Christ, and start walking with Him, let's not fool ourselves. Right is right, and wrong is wrong. Even though we are Christians, we can fall into a hole. We can make mistakes. It is then that James speaks to us, "Cleanse your hands, ye sinners."

How can believers cleanse their hands? This is not difficult. "Confess your sins." He is faithful and just to forgive you. When we repent of our sinfulness and admit that we are unprofitable servants, we must first of all forsake the things that are wrong. We must turn to the things that are right. We must be honest with ourselves, and quit doing what is wrong.

"Purify your hearts, ye double-minded." What does James mean by "double-minded"? Being of two minds — thinking of self, and thinking of Christ. Thinking of Christ and thinking of self. Thinking that we are doing what Christ wants us to do, and all the time, planning what we want to do. As a result we are in confusion. We're trying to go north and south at the same time. We are trying to save our money and spend it at the same time. How many times are we in this kind of trouble because we are going both ways? That's being double-minded.

Now James says to us, "Purify your heart." How can this be done? There is no trick to it. The answer is as plain as this: deny yourself, and turn to the Lord. That will take care of it. "Be afflicted, and mourn and weep." Whatever in the world we do, we should never be casual about this. Let us not deceive ourselves with the idea that becoming a "hail fellow, well met" will make everything all right with us. If we do wrong, if we live wrong in the sight of God, we have one foot in a bear trap, as sure as we live. There is no use acting coy about it. There is no use covering up. We're simply caught in a hole — but we can get out! Certainly we can get out!

"Let your laughter be turned to mourning, and your joy to heaviness," — let us sorrow and mourn for our wrong doing from the bottom of our hearts. If we have neglected the Lord, if we have not gone to church to worship God, but have spent His day going our own way, let us sorrow over our sins. Let us not deceive ourselves. "Whatsoever a man soweth, that shall he also reap" (Galatians 6:7). If we belong to Him, let us walk in His way and we will be blessed. If we walk in our own selfish way, and others seem to think that we are all right — this does not make it so. We Christians face a cunning foe, who schemes to undo everything we have that is good. He wants to undo and destroy us through our natural interests and our natural tendencies to sin. We all have the tendency to be downright self-indulgent. We are selfish and proud. When we fall into these traps James says to us, "Resist the devil, and he will flee from you." Turn to God. "Cleanse your hands, ye sinners; purify your hearts, ye double-minded. Be afflicted, and mourn, and weep: let your laughter be turned to mourning, and your joy to heaviness. Humble yourselves in the sight of the Lord, and he shall lift you up." Christian! You need not live a defeated life. Come to God in humility. God will lift you up.

Chapter 34

DO NOT JUDGE OTHERS

> Speak not evil one of another, brethren. He that speaketh evil of his brother, and judgeth his brother, speaketh evil of the law, and judgeth the law: but if thou judge the law, thou art not a doer of the law, but a judge. There is one lawgiver, who is able to save and to destroy: who art thou that judgest another? (James 4:11, 12).

The human heart is sinful and leads a person into wicked ways. Sin in general centers all thought and action upon self. It is natural for any man to evaluate every situation in terms of his own advantage: I want to do what I like and what I think will serve me and my plans.

One of my problems is other people. Often they seem to want what I want. If they succeed in getting what they want, I may have to get along without what I want. So I enter into competition and try to get ahead of others so I can get mine first before they have a chance to get theirs.

To be sure to get ahead of others I will do what I can to hinder them. An easy way to make it hard for my rival is to say things about him that will cause others to avoid helping him, or even to work against him because he is as bad as I say he is. James calls this "speaking evil of one another," and he warns Christians to control their human disposition to talk against others in the mistaken notion that they can thus advance their own interests.

In his discussion of the practice of speaking "evil of one another" James points out that in this practice a person is going contrary to the law of God. Moses had clearly set forth laws

137

and judgments that would guide the people of God to be considerate of each other's welfare, and to be charitable to the poor. At no point was self-interest approved. "Thou shalt love thy neighbor as thyself" was the plain thrust of the law of God.

James warned believers that only God was authorized to judge anyone. When a Christian begins to speak about anyone to the hurt of that person, he has actually judged that person as unworthy of help or support and has proposed that punishment should be handed out. Such judgment belongs only to God. He alone has the authority to condemn.

The law was given to be the guide to the believer. Its primary purpose is to show me the nature of my own actions, and to guide me into what would be pleasing to God. It was never intended to be used by me in measuring the acts or conduct of another person. When I use it that way I am taking God's place as Judge. James would warn me against presumption in using the law to find fault in others.

James does not offer any long argument to show that no Christian is worthy to judge his brother. He simply challenges the believer to consider who he really is. When any Christian looks at himself he knows he is a sinner saved by the grace of God. And since he is a sinner in his own heart and life he certainly is not fit to judge anyone else for not being all he ought to be.

Here again we can see how James undertakes to help his readers into richer experiences in believing. Recognizing that sinful practices will hinder blessing James writes to expose these practices so that the Christian can be delivered from them. While it is true that the Christian has natural sinful tendencies in his human nature, James is remembering that the believer is given the grace of God "to will and to do of His good pleasure."

Chapter 35

DO NOT COUNT ON TIME

> Go to now, ye that say, Today or tomorrow we will go into
> such a city, and continue there a year, and buy and sell, and
> get gain: whereas ye know not what shall be on the morrow
> (James 4:13, 14a).

James speaks plainly as he sets forth the truth of everyday living. If James had given a name for this letter, which he wrote himself, he could have called it, "Plain talk about Christian living." He writes realistically, calling a spade a spade. He speaks forcefully and sometimes bluntly. He saves time and words by stating his ideas simply and directly. Can we appreciate that his reason for doing this is that he is kind, that he wants to help us? The only reason he points out the boil on the back of the neck is that he can also point to the cure.

James has a way of simply opening up any situation so that daylight shows through. This is how he writes regarding "time." In this passage James reminds us how foolish it is for anyone to make great plans, because he does not know what is going to happen tomorrow. And isn't it true that even as we plan for the next day, as far as we are concerned, we cannot manage what we have in hand right now? We do not get done the very things we need to do right now! Why should we think that we will do better tomorrow? After all, we are just human, and in many ways just that foolish. Thinking that we will do better tomorrow does not make it so.

James would ask us to open our eyes, because this way of thinking is not God's way. We may when looking at tomorrow ask, What shall we do? The answer found in the Old Testament is still true. "Trust in the Lord and do good. Rest in him. Wait also on him. He shall bring it to pass" (Psalm 37). I used to teach school and for a while I was Professor at Seminary. Believe it or not, even when men get to the place where they are preparing for the ministry, they have the same problem they had when they were school children about getting the work done. It was often a real task to get it done on time. How often these men were given assignments which they did not do promptly. First thing they knew they were behind in their work. Anyone of my former students may remember and recognize this oft-repeated warning: "If you can't keep up, how are you going to catch up?" In other words, if I couldn't get anything done today why should I think that I am going to get everything done tomorrow? How foolish of me to make big plans for tomorrow, when actually today I am making blunders and mistakes!

James would say, "Brother, get wise. Get next to yourself. Wake up. What makes you think you can do tomorrow what you cannot do today?" Actually when we are making our plans of what we will do next week, we are counting that we will be here well and able. How do we know that we will not be in the hospital or have a broken leg? Our planning is so normal, so natural, but in reality we cannot guarantee that we will be here. We even plan for next month and next year. We always assume that we will be allowed to proceed. This is not unusual, and yet we cannot control the things that happen. No man knows what a day will bring forth.

James is warning us that projecting our plans on uncertain ground can lead to disaster, and usually does. Many big plans have resulted in sorrow and grief. Some of us are so foolish that we even borrow money on the strength of our big plans. We always figure that everything is going to work out just fine — we will always be healthy, we will always have our job. We will always be fortunate. We will never lose anything or have an accident. How foolish can we be? Our actual appraisal of our conduct and procedure, ridiculous as it sounds, is based deep down in our hearts in vanity and self-confidence.

Every now and again someone will claim that self-confidence is good, because it gets things done. It may be true from a practical point of view that it does get things started. But from a

Christian's point of view this is foolish. Believers can do better than that. Instead of putting their trust in themselves, they could put their trust in God. Proudly in our self-assurance we may speak and think of the big things we will do tomorrow. When we couldn't do it today, what makes us think we can do it tomorrow? A person may be so willful in self-will. He is going to plan, he is going to do, he has the situation well in hands! He is going to accomplish it! Can he really be sure? James would urge us to be humble.

It is so common for men to plan without regard to God. They just hope when they make their plans that God will let them get by. Often they know that they are not able to accomplish their plans but they feel that He will just naturally help them. It never dawns on them that God will judge them before He helps them. Just because God is almighty and merciful and gracious does not mean that He approves or will support all they do. God is too gracious and too wise to approve everything men plan and do. But if Christians put their trust in Him, if they seek to know His mind, they can be led. James would say, "Wake up brother, open your eyes! Look up to God. Let God have His way in your life. Then it will make no difference about tomorrow. With God you have eternity!"

Chapter 36

FRAILTY OF LIFE

> For what is your life? It is even a vapour, that appeareth for
> a little time, and then vanisheth away. For that ye ought to
> say, If the Lord will, we shall live, and do this, or that. But
> now ye rejoice in your boastings: all such rejoicing is evil
> (James 4:14b-16).

In these earnest words James stresses the truth that human
life is frail and uncertain. He begins by raising a question, "What
is your life?" What does it amount to? And then proceeds to
point out that life is easily wiped out and ended.

Any person who has seen someone die or has lost a loved one
is conscious of the fact that life is frail. Sometimes when an
extremely sick person dies, it is actually a relief to see the end
of his suffering. Sometimes a person may die in his sleep. I
can remember looking into the face of our baby, seventeen
months old, lying in his crib just as if he had fallen asleep. His
face looked normal, just quiet and still, but dead. It was almost
impossible to believe that moments before he had been breathing,
and now he was gone. Just a breath!

We may remember when we were children having leaned on
some window sill and blown our breath on the glass just to see
it fade away. James compares this to life when he says, "What
is your life? It is even a vapour" (just a little mist) "that ap-
peareth for a little time, and then vanisheth away." How frail
we are! We cannot prolong our life by a heart beat. When our
time comes and God calls us, our hearts will stop beating and
we will be gone. On the basis of this James goes on to say:
"For that ye ought to say, If the Lord will, we shall live, and do

this, or that." In view of the weakness of our lives, in view of the frailty of our life that is within us, we should never talk so confidently about what we are going to do tomorrow. We ought rather to say: "If the Lord will, we shall live, and do this, or that."

My father was not what would be called a pious man. As a matter of fact, in all my childhood days, my father was not a man who professed to be a Christian. He tried to live a good, honest life; he tried to be reliable; but I could not say that I ever got the impression that he trusted God. He believed there was a God. He thought that God would judge him, and on the basis of that judgment, he expected to be condemned. He thought this would be right and just, for he deserved it. And yet he was not a man who led us in praying, and he did not personally offer prayer to God in my hearing, during my boyhood days. But whenever he would be making plans for the next day or the next week, he would so often include this phrase, "Well, if we live, we'll do this. If we live, we'll do that." When we were making plans for the coming year on the farm, he would use these words. That was his way of saying just what James has in mind here. James worded it a little differently: "If the Lord will, we shall live, and do this, or that."

In verse 16 James continues, "But now ye rejoice in your boastings: all such rejoicing is evil." How do we rejoice in our boastings? of what do we boast? We boast of tomorrow: we boast about what we are going to do. We boast that we will be here. We are making a big point of something that isn't true yet, something that we are expecting. In our expectation, we expect to be here, and to be able. We expect, in fact to be a little stronger and a little smarter than we are now. We give ourselves credit for growing, for improving, and so we expect to be here and do these things. James would say, "That's all a mistake. You cannot guarantee that you will be here, so don't talk that way. Don't make those big plans for what you will do next week, or five years from now."

We could be considered impudent and arrogant for making plans over which we have no control. God has control of these things. If we want to talk honestly and intelligently we should say, "If the Lord wills, we will do this, or we will do that." This is very important. If He will allow His strength to be in us, and His grace to watch over us, certain things could follow. Christians should give God the glory, because in doing so they admit that life and strength, protecting care, all come from Him. As surely as we give God the glory it will keep us humble. Talking about the future, planning for it as though it were in our hands, tends to make us arrogant and tends to strengthen our pride all the way around, and this is evil.

When we assume that tomorrow we'll do some great things, because we are smart and strong, we are not thinking soundly. This is not wholesome and it is not good. In fact it is evil. Why is it evil? Because we are imposing on God. We are planning something we do not have. We are actually presuming upon God. When we do this it tends to make us smug, and proud and vain. We are going to make plans. We are going to accomplish things! All this kind of thinking makes us independent in a bad way. We will not be thankful to God. Regardless of whether we are pleasing to God, we will do as we please. Since we do not know what the day will bring forth, we should walk softly before God. We should walk humbly before Him, in order that He may bless us. We should leave all our tomorrows in His hand.

Chapter 37

DEFINITION OF SIN

Therefore to him that knoweth to do good, and doeth it not,
to him it is sin (James 4:17).

All of us have thought at different times about that word "sin."
It is only a little three letter word, s-i-n, and in this day and
time people do not talk much about sin. "Sin" actually has no
meaning unless we know God. If one has no idea of God, one
wouldn't have any idea of sin. If God means nothing to us, sin
means nothing to us. That little word, "sin," refers to any action,
or any conduct, which is not like God.

When people say today there is little sense of sin, they may
not realize that this is so because there is so little sense of God.
People do not think about God; they do not talk about God.
People who do not think about God, do not think about sin.
People who are not conscious of God, are not conscious of sin.
Those who have a keen sense of God, have a keen sense of sin.
Sometimes people will say, "Well, I'd be conscious of sin, if I
did something very bad, something really wrong." Not necessarily! There are some whose lives are literally wicked, who never
give sin a second thought. If they can get away with it everything is just fine as far as they are concerned. Sin does not turn
against itself: sin doesn't cause anyone to feel badly. As a matter
of fact, sin feels good to human nature, and to human beings.

To understand sin we have to start by thinking about God, because sin is opposite from God. The Catechism uses these words:
"Sin is any want of conformity unto, or transgression of, the
Law of God." This is an excellent description so far as the law
is concerned, and from that point of view. Now in colloquial

145

language of people such as we are, we would say, "anything not like God is sin."

The Law of God is an outward description of what His nature is, and of how God really sees things. If we do not go by the Law, we do not keep the ten commandments. When we break them, we commit sin. In the second chapter of the book of James, we had another description of sin which fits in along the lines we have been talking about. "Whosoever shall keep the whole law, and yet offend in one point, he is guilty of all." In this we see that with reference to the requirements of the Law we are sinners, even if we sin only once in our life. When we first think of sin we are inclined to feel that the word "sinner" ought to be kept for people who sin over and over again. But this is not the case. It would be a rather gruesome thing to be asked, "How many men would you have to kill to be a murderer?" Obviously, killing one man would make a man a murderer, and just so, committing one sin would make any man a sinner.

But in the verse we are now considering (James 4:17) James presents an even more profound definition for sin. "Therefore to him that knoweth to do good, and doeth it not, to him it is sin." This is not really any different from what we have read before. It spells out a little more clearly that to do good is God's way. If we know to do good and do it not, this is sin, because it is not at all like God. This means that the sin of commission is no more real than the sin of omission. We can do wrong, by doing wrong, and we can do wrong, by doing nothing. If we saw a man drowning in a canal and did nothing, it would be wrong. If we saw a child running out in the street in front of an oncoming truck, and did nothing about it, that would be wrong. If someone were crossing a railroad track and he did not see the train coming, and we did not warn him, it would be wrong. In other words, if we know to do good and do it not, we sin. This is saying in a more specific way that want of conformity unto or transgression of the Law of God is sin. Clearly then, if a situation arises where we have an opportunity to do good, but we don't "do good," that would be wrong, that would be sin. We are not like God, when we sit down instead of going somewhere to do good: when we drop out when we could take part in doing that which is good.

Thus it is sin if we do not worship God. We all know perfectly well that we live our life around the clock, and around the week. We live from Sunday to Sunday through all the days of the week. Somewhere on Sunday people gather to worship God. Should we go? Yes! Do we go? No! What's that? Sin! We cannot say, "But I didn't do anything." The fact that we did nothing, was sin. Take the matter of reading the Bible. Should we read the Bible? Yes! If we do not read the Bible — it's sin. Take the matter of prayer. Should we pray? Yes! When we do not pray we sin.

If we see an opportunity to help others and do not help, that's wrong. If we see people who should be respected and honored, and we do not respect them, that's wrong. We need not do anything against them: not considering them, not respecting them is wrong. If we live to ourselves and never do anything for anyone else, that is not the way it should be. When we know to do good in helping people, and we don't do it, we have sinned.

Again let us consider the matter of giving. When we do not give to the United Appeal, to the Community Chest, or to the Red Cross — that's wrong. We cannot say, "We didn't do anything," as though that were an excuse. When we didn't do anything, that was sin.

If we do not seek God's face, if we do not take time to pray, if we do not go to church to worship God, nor read the Word of God that we might come to know it, all of that is sin. "Therefore to him that knoweth to do good, and doeth it not, to him it is sin." So, if we know something that would help our neighbor, we should do it. As far as people in our home are concerned, no matter how they have acted, if we know what would be good for them, we should do it. So far as our own souls are concerned, if Bible reading and prayer would make us more like the Lord Jesus we should do it. Because if we neglect our souls God would count it as sin.

Chapter 38

MISERIES OF THE RICH

Go to now, ye rich men, weep and howl for your miseries
that shall come upon you. Your riches are corrupted, and your
garments are moth-eaten. Your gold and silver is cankered; and
the rust of them shall be a witness against you, and shall eat
your flesh as it were fire. Ye have heaped treasure together for
the last days (James 5:1-3).

Our first reaction as we read these words is one of shock.
Our next thought would be that riches are dangerous, that it is
actually risky to be rich. All this James implies as he addresses
people whom he calls rich, who trust in their riches. The word,
"rich," is in itself a relative word. We could be rich when we
are with one company of people, but the same assets would not
be considered "rich" in another company of people. So the word
"rich" is actually a relative term. For anyone who feels he is rich
it doesn't make any difference how much money he has. Just
having the feeling that we are rich, or smart or strong or powerful, makes us rich. Anything that gives us an advantage over
other people makes us rich. It could be money, it could be
friends, it could be family.

We could be born into a certain family, and feel that we are
better than anyone else. This would make us feel rich. We
could belong to a certain race, and because we belong to that
race, we might think that we are better than other people. It
could be that we have a certain college degree, which makes
us feel superior over other people. It could be that we feel rich
in physical strength. Being more handsome or beautiful than
anyone else in a family would normally make us feel rich.

Now apparently the evil involved here is in putting our trust in what we consider riches. When we trust in riches, whatever they may be, rather than trusting in God, that's evil. As a matter of fact, when we trust in riches, instead of trusting God, that's idolatry. It means that we are putting our trust in something less than God.

To gain a better understanding of these verses we turn to Matthew 6:19 - 21. These verses in Matthew are so similar to the verses in James that we may assume that Matthew and James heard the same things from the lips of the same Master and Teacher. Matthew records the words of the Lord Jesus: "Lay not up for yourselves treasures upon earth, where moth and rust doth corrupt, and where thieves break through and steal: but lay up for yourselves treasures in heaven, where neither moth nor rust doth corrupt, and where thieves do not break through nor steal" (Matthew 6:19, 20). James writes, "Your riches are corrupted, and your garments are moth-eaten. Your gold and silver is cankered; and the rust of them shall be a witness against you, and shall eat your flesh as it were fire. Ye have heaped treasure together for the last days" (James 5:2, 3). When we put our trust in riches, when we gather riches together and hoard them like a miser, we are in grave danger. The rich young ruler provides an illustration of this. When the Lord Jesus told him to give his money to the poor, he went away sorrowfully, because he had great possessions.

For a Christian there is one safe way to have riches. There is one way in which we can have many friends, or belong to a very good family and yet be blessed. There is one way in which we can belong to a fortunate race, and not be handicapped, one safe way in which we can have a good education and not be spoiled by it. There is a safe way in which we can be physically strong or beautiful. For all these things there is only one safe way for a Christian to keep himself from contamination with the things that give him an advantage over others — by using these advantages on behalf of the people who do not have them. If we use our assets, which give us the advantage over others, for the benefit of others we will have chosen the safe way. If we happen to have money, we are not necessarily expected to give it all away, so that we will be poor too. Instead the meaning is that we will not use our money only for ourselves, but that we will share it with those who are in need. When we have a great many friends we should not visit only with them. This could become a snare to us. It could make us selfish and self-centered. Instead of that we should make it a point to hunt out those people in the congregation who do not have friends: call on the woman who knows no one, visit in her home and spend some time with her; be friendly with a person who belongs to a race that is less fortunate than yours; go to that person and actually show him that you want to help him in every possible way. You need not live in that person's home, nor come down to any particular social level where he happens to be, but you should be interested in him and want to help him.

If I am well educated and understand things well, I will want to be kept from being proud and haughty and vain. If I want to be kept from looking down on other people, to deride and sneer at those who have no education, I need only to help them. Then my education will prove a blessing. If I am strong, I should spend some time with the person who is weak. By exercising myself in behalf of the less fortunate, the person who does not have advantages, my own advantages will be kept clean.

We must remember that James is writing to us, who are Christians, in order that we may be blessed. Being a Christian does not make us rich, just as becoming a Christian does not make us members of the same family and social status. Just because we are Christians, this does not make us owners of shops. It does not make everyone manager of a store. Just because we are Christians, it does not mean that we will all become Generals. Nothing like that! I may as a Christian continue to be a housewife. As a Christian I may be a person with money, with a lovely home and a good car. I may be a person who has advantage over other people. James has a dire warning for the rich. "Do not let your riches ruin you spiritually." To be fortunate and rich is to be "on the spot" spiritually speaking. A man could get spiritually hurt by having earthly riches.

Chapter 39

FRAUD IS NOTED BY GOD

Behold, the hire of the labourers who have reaped down your fields, which is of you kept back by fraud, crieth: and the cries of them which have reaped are entered into the ears of the Lord of Sabaoth (James 5:4).

These words seem very simple, and yet their message is obscure. It is the kind of Scripture one could read and pass by. A person could feel that he is in favor of it, and let it go at that. It would be easy to ignore the message.

The figure that is involved here is that of old-time farming. In this reference the laborers had been in the field and had reaped the crops, whereas the farmer had cheated them about their wages. He had contracted to pay them a certain amount; and then when the work was done he would not pay the wages he had agreed to pay. Because he was rich and they were poor, because he owned the place and they didn't, he could order them off and they had to leave. "The cries of them which have reaped are entered into the ears of the Lord of Sabaoth." When a man mistreats his employees, when he takes advantage of some humble field worker, God sees and God will judge him.

How true it is in human affairs that the rich get richer. It seems obvious that money makes money. As a young man, when I first observed these things around me, I felt the unfairness of it. The man who has the cash and can afford what he wants can buy for less, because with cash he can get a discount. A rich man pays cash for his car. Another man buys on time, and pays not only his monthly payments but as much interest on top of that as the law will allow. There is something about this that seems not quite fair.

This same principle works on other levels. Those of us who have gone to college have seen it there; many a time the smart student can get by with poor preparation because he is smart. He can even get good grades in an examination without much effort. This sort of thing happens over and over again. In your community a man may get a traffic ticket, or he may be in trouble because of a shady deal. How often is heard the expression, "Well, if you just know Joe you'll be all right." What does that mean? It means simply that if you know someone who can put you in touch with the person who can fix things for a price you do not need to pay the full amount. And so in this area of dishonest dealings as well, the man with the money wins out.

The poor man is obliged to pay higher interest rates. The rich man can borrow at a lower rate. All this violates basic equity. It is not fair, but as far as this world is concerned it is going to happen. Some time ago I heard of a man who was able to borrow money from the government because he could make the down payment for some property. He built houses with the borrowed money, sold them at a profit, and then repaid the government. This man did nothing dishonest, but his money gave him a big advantage. A poor man who did not have the money, who had no collateral, could never raise the money to produce a product that could give him a profit. This is true in the business world.

As far as we as Christians are concerned, we should be extremely careful about using our advantages. These advantages are derived from other people. If we find things easy at a certain point along the way, they are easy for us only because someone else carried the load. Someone else did the heavy work in order to get this thing done.

James would say that when a man owns a farm and hires laborers to do the work, the tendency of that man is to take advantage of the poor. In our day this condition has brought on various devices which try to correct the situation. We now see workers banding themselves together so that as a group they may make certain demands as far is their pay is concerned. I personally have grave misgivings about the fact that now we pay a man by the hour rather than according to the work he does.

Despite such controls the general situation is much the same as it was in the time of James. With the rich, with those who have money, and authority, and position, and power there is still the tendency to take advantage of the poor. Let the yardman go the extra step, keep the maid overtime and make her do extra work without extra pay. This is the tendency. Christians need to take to heart that God sees this. Let us be careful that we never take advantage of the poor. God has an eye on them. He will deal with us· in judgment if we do not treat them well.

Chapter 40

WICKED HAVE OPPRESSED

> Ye have lived in pleasure on the earth, and been wanton; ye have nourished your hearts, as in a day of slaughter. Ye have condemned and killed the just; and he doth not resist you (James 5:5, 6).

This Scripture sets forth words of heavy indictment. James gives expression here to the judgment of God. He shows in these words how Almighty God feels about everything that is involved in His works and in His law. God cares about all people. He wants His people, those who trust in Him, to be blessed as they walk in His way.

It is hard to realize that James is writing to Christians. "Ye have lived in pleasure on the earth, and been wanton; ye have nourished your hearts, as in a day of slaughter. Ye have condemned and killed the just; and he doth not resist you." This is his description of people who have taken advantage of others. The stern words of verse 4 are expanded in verses 5 and 6. The world, of course, would demand that Christians should be perfect. But this is really not the world's business. Actually, the world has it own score to settle. Yet so far as we are concerned, as Christians we should keep this in mind, so that we can understand James.

When I became a Christian, that did not mean that I was changed into an angel; and when you became a Christian, that did not mean that you were changed into an angel. Actually all of us can grow in truth and grace to become more and more like the Lord Jesus Christ. But we don't start that way. The Law still prevails so far as we are concerned. When we as Christians sin God's judgment will be upon us. The believer who sins will lose. He will lose his joy. He will lose his blessing. There are Christian people who are not happy. There are Christian people who are barren and empty. There are those who are weak, without strength.

When Christians confess their sins Christ Jesus is faithful and just to forgive and to cleanse them from all unrighteousness. This is the truth! If the believer will confess his sins all will be well.

A selfish Christian looks like a selfish agnostic. A selfish Christian will act just like a selfish unbeliever. He will be interested in himself. A cruel believer will act just like any other cruel man. Just because he is a Christian he will not receive any special preferential treatment from God. If he is cruel he will be dealt with according to his cruelty. If he is selfish he will be treated according to his selfishness. The Apostle Paul had these things in mind when he wrote of Christians whose works were "wood, hay and stubble" (I Corinthians 3:12). In the Day of Judgment their works will be consumed with fire, although their soul would be saved, "though as by fire." The works that they did were worthless.

When James uses the words, "Ye have lived in pleasure," he does not define in what area. He does not define on what level. His words may include that you lived in pleasure physically. You have enjoyed yourself, eating and drinking, and doing the things you wanted to do. "You have lived in pleasure on the earth and been wanton." "Been wanton" is to say, you have been careless and profligate. You have allowed yourself to do anything you wanted to do. Maybe it was physical or maybe it was social. You just ran around with your crowd and you enjoyed doing everything they did, no matter what they did on Sunday, or Friday night, or on Wednesday night. Maybe there was prayer meeting Wednesday night over at the church but you did not go. Maybe there was a special meeting at church Saturday night. But that was the night you went to the football game. You just did anything you wanted to do. When Sunday came around you wanted to lie in bed. You just enjoyed staying in bed a little longer. "Ye have lived in pleasure . . . and been wanton," which means you lived carelessly.

Some of us may enjoy reading. We may take pleasure in our

arguments and in our reading. We read books that discuss all kinds of things. Books on whether to believe this part of the Bible or whether not to believe that part of the Bible, and all the time we believe nothing. God sees that. He knows perfectly well that we are just seeking and doing our own pleasure, as we read.

Some of us may have lived in pleasure in a political way. We are enjoying the fact that our party is in power. We have taken special privileges because we could have them, even if it meant taking advantage of other people. We have had all the time in the world for special meetings and have served on special committees. "We have lived in pleasure and been wanton."

I can do all this and yet be a Christian, but this is not the way a Christian should do things. I know I am a Christian when I believe in the Lord Jesus Christ. But even when I believe in the Lord Jesus Christ my old human nature will lead me out into these things.

"Ye have nourished your hearts, as in a day of slaughter." Unless we know how animals are prepared for food, we might have trouble understanding James at this point. We need to realize that steers are specially fed so that they will make good steaks. Hogs are specially fed to make good pork. Chickens and turkeys are specially fed to fatten them up for the table. James is saying, "You've pampered yourself in everything that you did." "Ye have nourished your hearts, as in a day of slaughter."

"Ye have condemned and killed the just; and he doth not resist you." You took advantage of the meek, the just, the humble man. You simply took advantage of him because he was humble, because he was meek. You went ahead with your own plans and did as you pleased.

Thus James has completed his description of the people who have been misled. He has completed his denouncement of the people who have wilfully sought their own pleasure. They have used their money and time in a way that has brought them harm. They have been tricked by their riches. In all of this the Christian can repent. He can turn to the Lord humbly and ask Him to forgive him in grace and mercy and to show him His way.

Chapter 41

PATIENCE WAITS WITH HOPE

> Be patient therefore, brethren, unto the coming of the Lord. Behold, the husbandman waiteth for the precious fruit of the earth, and hath long patience for it, until he receive the early and latter rain (James 5:7).

In telling Christians to be patient James uses the figure of the farmer who plants his grain in the Spring and then waits until harvest time to receive the results of his labors, the consequence of his action. As Christians we should live in obedience to the Lord. That is the way in which a Christian life is ordered. Oftentimes, the action which we take, when we are led by the Holy Spirit, does not bring immediate results that can be seen. When we turn aside on Sunday to go to church and worship God, feeling led by the Holy Spirit to do this, we have God's promise that He will bless us. God may not bless us that very afternoon. Our church attendance will not necessarily result in an immediate change in our fortunes, or our affairs. The blessing may come later. We are given assurance that when we follow the guidance of the Holy Spirit, blessing will come. Our home will be blessed, but this does not always come immediately. For this reason we need to be patient, when we have planted the seed, to wait and wait until harvest time comes.

To obey the laws of the land may seem very routine. There is not much imagination in just being an obedient good citizen. It is a rather prosaic way of living. We do not do anything exceptional when we do what is expected of us. But there are never ending benefits that will follow later. To receive the benefits we must continue to obey the laws of the land in being quiet, unassuming, faithful citizens.

Being considerate among the people with whom we live may sometimes seem to be a thankless job. We are thoughtful of other people who oftentimes are not thoughtful of us. When we do things for people who do nothing for us, we may appear rather slow-witted and ignorant. To be considerate of people who are never considerate of us would not be called smart by some people. As Christians we need to remember we are not trying to be smart. All we are trying to do is to be obedient to the inner guidance we have from the Lord.

To be sure the most menial tasks around the house can take on new meaning if they are done as unto the Lord. Thus our daily chores and our daily routine will no longer seem such a useless procedure. When we are considerate, obedient, and faithful in the things we do, because deep down in our hearts we are led to do the right thing, God Himself will bless us. Then the humblest daily routine will have a blessing attached to it. James says, "Be patient therefore, brethren, unto the coming of the Lord." It may take time but the Lord will come into every trying situation and He will do something about it to bring blessing.

This principle applies to the life of Christians anywhere. People of the world find that because they can depend on us to do certain things they can take advantage of us and let us do it all. We may receive no thanks from them for all the extra things we do. James would tell us in this situation to keep it up. "Be patient therefore." Remember, there will be results and there will be benefits, and there will be consequences, because they have been promised to us by the Lord whom we serve.

When we show our good will to people who work with us in the office and we go out of our way to show them consideration and courtesy, because we love the Lord, blessing attaches to this. James would say, "Keep it up. Stay with it. (Be patient therefore, brethren, unto the coming of the Lord). Go right on doing good, until the Lord Himself takes a hand."

It could be that few people in our community are interested in the appearance of the streets. When we do something to improve the appearance and the morale of our neighborhood we are being helpful to the people living around us. If we are being helpful because we are Christians we should never be discouraged even if no one seems to care or appreciate what we are doing, for we have been promised the blessing of God.

Sometimes giving to the poor seems an empty gesture. In giving to the poor day after day because we are being charitable we can become discouraged. We can get the feeling that we are putting our money into a bottomless hole. At such times we should remember that we have the promise of blessing. "He that giveth to the poor, lendeth to the Lord" (paraphrase of Proverbs 19:17). As surely as we are helpful to the poor, God will be helpful to us.

When James uses the words, "unto the coming of the Lord," he is urging us to keep on doing what God expects us to do. In due time God will take a hand and will reward us openly. "The coming of the Lord" in the writing of James is similar to "the day of the Lord" in the Old Testament prophets. The Day of the Lord will be apparently the day when the Lord appears in the situation and begins to act. Often as we are being faithful in our lives and in our individual places of service, we have the feeling that no one cares. We feel as though we are walking along under a gray sky with no break in it. James is assuring us that one day the clouds will lift and the sun will burst through.

"The coming of the Lord draweth nigh" (James 5:8b). The Lord Himself will take over and begin to act. Christians can very well keep in mind that there is a great day coming. "The Lord will one day show Himself strong on behalf of those who put their trust in Him" (paraphrase of II Chronicles 16:9). The purpose of this portion of James is to impress these very words upon our hearts. "Be patient therefore." Stick to it, brother, unto the coming of the Lord. "Behold, the husbandman waits for the precious fruit of the earth, he hath long patience for it, until he receive the early and latter rain." Things must happen in succession, the seed time and the waiting until the time of the harvest. Eventually the Lord will come. When we put our trust in Him, when we are faithful to Him, when we are helpful to those around us, we can be sure that God's blessing will certainly be ours.

Chapter 42

PATIENCE AWAITS THE COMING OF THE LORD

Be ye also patient; stablish your hearts: for the coming of the
Lord draweth nigh (James 5:8).

In verse 7 James used the illustration of the farmer who plants
his garden in the Spring and waits for the harvest. He waits
patiently through the various seasons, until the early and the
latter rain come, until the time when he can reap his grain in
the Fall and receive the consequences and the results of his labor
and his time of waiting. James says, "Be ye also patient, in your
Christian life and experience."

In many aspects in our lives as Christians we are like the
farmer. Doing the things that would please the Lord, obeying
Him and doing His will, are much like sowing the seed. The
results of this may not occur at once. We might have to wait.
"Be ye also patient; stablish your hearts: for the coming of the
Lord draweth nigh." In all that is revealed about the will of
God and about God's dealing with men, we are taught to look
forward to one thing: there will be a day of harvest. In everything that happens in this world there will be a showdown.

The truth of the coming showdown is to be seen in the parable
of the sower and the seed. The climax of the parable is the
time of fruition, the time of harvest, when some seed brought
forth twenty-fold, some thirty-fold, some sixty-fold, some hun-
dred-fold. It is in the time of harvest that the consequences are
revealed.

This same truth is shown in the parable of the wheat and the
tares. The wheat and the tares grew up together and then came

the time of harvest. It was then the separation took place. The wheat was gathered in and the tares were burned.

Just so in the parable of the net when the fishermen threw the net out into the lake to catch fish. As they brought the net to land with a great many fish, they found that the net contained good fish and bad fish. They separated them. They threw away the bad fish and kept the good fish.

This truth is shown again in the parable of the talents. The master gave talents to his servants before he left on a far journey. He gave five talents to one servant, to another he gave two talents, and to another he gave one talent. When the master returned there was a day of report. This was the showdown. This was the day of judgment. The servants brought in their results, their reports, and they were judged accordingly.

Again in the parable of the wicked servant who thought his master would not return so soon, we find him beating his fellow servants. The point in this parable is that the master did come and brought that servant to judgment in a showdown.

Consider the very significant parable of the ten virgins. Five were ready for the bridegroom, five were not. The real difference did not show up until the bridegroom came and all were faced with a showdown. When the bridegroom came the five who were wise and had oil in their lamps went into the banquet hall with him. The five foolish virgins who were not prepared were left outside, but the door was closed. They never did get in.

Once more there is the parable of the sheep and the goats. These were not separated until the day of judgment. They represent people who lived and worked along together and came together to the day of judgment for the showdown. Then came the time of separation. Those who had done the will of God were separated to be blessed from those who had followed their own way, who now were turned away from blessing.

All these parables so briefly noted point to one truth. It is sure and certain that everything moves to a showdown. There will be a day when the facts will come out. Since there is this day of fulfillment approaching for all of us James would say, "Stick to the service of the Lord. Stick to being obedient. Have patience; stablish your hearts."

The word "stablish" has in it the idea of "build it solid and sure, put a good foundation under it." We believe in God, let us work that way. Act that way. Count on it. Think about it. Pray about it.

Do we believe in God's promises? Do we truly believe that God will do what He said He would do? We can be sure that there will be a day of the big showdown.

We know that a time will come when God will manifest His power, so let us be wise and let us put our trust in Him now. We establish our hearts by believing all His promises. When we take a deliberate grip on the promises of the Lord, and we trust Him to carry them out, He will bless us.

Our future is unknown to us but when we are in the will of God and trusting in Him, believing in the Lord Jesus Christ, we may be confident of how it will be. It will be glorious! "Be ye also patient; stablish your hearts." When we think of the things of the Lord Jesus Christ, when we call to mind the truths of the Bible as we read it, we are stablishing our hearts. When we have a season of prayer in which we grow nigh to Him He will certainly be with us to bless us.

"For the coming of the Lord draweth nigh." There is this promise that the Lord will come. As far as we are concerned we know that the Lord Jesus Christ is alive. We know that Christ Jesus came into this world and was here for some thirty-three years. He was crucified and buried and His body was raised from the dead. All this we hold to be true. We also believe that He ascended into heaven in full view of many witnesses and that one day He will return.

"This same Jesus . . . shall return in like manner as ye have seen Him go" (paraphrase of Acts 1:11). All Christians from that day to this day have been told that the Lord will return. He will come again and bring the will of God to pass to the glory of His Name. This promise of Christ's return should at all times be in our hearts and minds. It will help us to be patient. To be ready for that day we will nurture our convictions and put our whole confidence in God. We will trust in the Providence of God that He will work things out well. We will trust in the Holy Spirit that He will guide us well, "for the coming of the Lord draweth nigh." It is getting closer and closer to the time when the Lord Jesus will reveal Himself. When we wonder about the time of His return we can keep in mind that we are nineteen hundred years closer to it now than when this was written.

James urges all Christians, "Be ye also patient" — as the farmer. Commit your way to the Lord in your attitude toward other people, in your attitude to the poor, and in all things, and then wait. While you are waiting trust His promises. Remember that even though you wait a long time, the Lord Jesus Christ will return. Knowing this, knowing that the Lord will return, Christians can afford to be patient and stablish their hearts. As far as their feelings are concerned they can comfort themselves with His promises. When they have fears they can comfort themselves by remembering His faithfulness. If they have any questions they can comfort themselves in the assurance that some day they shall know the answers. As surely as their hearts and minds are occupied with these thoughts, God will bless them. This is the promise of God, "The coming of the Lord draweth nigh." May God Himself prepare our hearts for that day.

Chapter 43

GRUDGE NOT

Grudge not one against another, brethren, lest ye be condemned: behold, the judge standeth before the door (James 5:9).

There are various translations of this verse, but all bring out the same line of thought. One of these translations is: "My brothers, do not blame your troubles on one another, or you will fall under judgment; and there stands the Judge, at the door" *(New English Bible).* Another translator writes, "Do not complain against one another, brothers, so that God will not judge you" *(Today's English Version).* This brings out the thought that when we complain against people God hears our complaint. Also it implies that the person who does the complaining may be the very one who is at fault. Another version reads, "Do not complain, brethren, against one another, so that you [yourselves] may not be judged. Look! The Judge is [already] standing at the very door" *(The Amplified New Testament).* Warning us that we are on the verge of being called into His presence to be judged should make us very careful how we judge others. Still another Greek scholar interprets this verse to mean, "Don't make complaints against each other in the meantime, my brothers — you may be the one at fault yourself. The judge himself is already at the door" (Phillips).

These various translations present an admonition that comes close to the hearts of all of us who are Christians, who are believers. Unbelievers would not pay attention to these words. Many preachers and teachers speak as though everyone in the world were listening to them. The call to repentance does go out to everyone. The invitation of God is to "all who will come," but many do not turn to God. For such people no particular message is being given. They would not listen to it anyway. God has other ways of dealing with them.

For us who are believers, who will listen, the message contained in this verse is written for our learning, "Grudge not one against another." Don't make complaints against one another. In other words, don't be fault finding all the time, lest you be the very one at fault. This matter of finding fault with other people is like a weed in the garden, and what a common weed it is. Carping and fault-finding can become a habit, and it's a mean habit. Living along, day by day, any one of us has to face things that are not easy. Daily routine can be wearisome. It can be monotonous and tiresome for a housewife to do the same things over and over again. A day's work at the plant can be a heavy task. Punching those typewriter keys can get to be old stuff. Even handling a computer can get to be a routine matter. In addition to the wearisome daily routine, there is the fact that every now and again we make mistakes. Things go wrong. We have calamities of one sort or another, and are tempted to look for someone to blame for our mistakes. When anything we do goes wrong, we quickly look around for a scapegoat.

Sometimes our hopes are in vain and disappointing. We look forward to certain results and these may not happen. When our hopes do not materialize we feel that someone hindered us and we become critical of other people. We feel that if everyone else had done his part our hopes could have been fulfilled. Things we had intended to do may fail. They may not work out. When such failures happen it is such an easy thing to look around for someone to blame.

As Christians we must not find fault with others. "Grudge not one against another." Someone may be to blame, but as these authors and translators say, "that someone may be you or I." Let us not blame anyone else — because we ourselves could be blamed. If we keep in mind that the judge is already at the door, we will not be so ready to blame others while we ourselves are under judgment. Even as we live our life in the presence of God, we can be in danger of finding fault with other people. Let us always remember that God looks right into us. He knows our very thoughts. They are as plain to Him as day. While we are criticizing others the Judge of all men may call us to account any time. This should cause us to go slowly when it comes to finding fault with other people.

When we are at work or at play, in the office or on the campus, and are on the verge of finding fault with someone, let us remember that the Judge is standing right at the door. He may come in to see us at any moment, and as surely as He looks at us we will be quite conscious then of the faults we have. The Lord may come or we may be called into His presence at any time. We have no positive assurance that we will see the end of this day, or the next daybreak. It's foolish for us to count on tomorrow.

We ought to live our life as it comes, when it comes and where it comes. In this way we can actually have dealings with God. Let us not fall into the habit of finding fault with other people "lest ye be condemned." "Behold, the judge standeth before the door." He is right close at hand. He is just ready to come in. We Christians expect God to judge the world and He will surely judge us. As Christians we think that as far as our homes are concerned God is the Head. So far as life is concerned God is here with us. So it behooves us to walk softly in His presence. We ought to realize that what we are saying and doing is subject to review by the Master, that Almighty God Himself is right here to see us as we act and do. Knowing this should affect us in such a way that we will be very careful not to judge other people nor to find fault with them.

If we pay no attention to these words we will be unhappy Christians. We will be poor Christians. If we seek the fullness of God's blessing upon us James will help us by hoeing out one weed after another. In this passage with a few verses for this and a few verses for that he is putting pressure on us to hoe out these weeds in our lives and to yield ourselves to God. The weeds we are hoeing out with verse 9 are fault-finding, holding grudges, blaming other people. We need to remember that God will put that very same principle to work so far as we are concerned. If we really want to help ourselves we will be gracious and merciful to others. Then God will grant His grace and mercy unto us.

Chapter 44

EXAMPLE OF THE PROPHETS

> Take, my brethren, the prophets, who have spoken in the name of the Lord, for an example of suffering affliction, and of patience (James 5:10).

Actually the meaning in these words could be more clear if we were to say, "patience while suffering affliction." In another translation we read, "an example of suffering an ill-treatment together with patience" *(Amplified)*. Still another Greek scholar has translated this passage to mean, "examples of patient endurance under suffering" *(Today's English Version)*. Another one writes, "a pattern of patience under ill-treatment . . ." *(New English Bible)*. And one more, "our example of the patient endurance of suffering . . ." *(Phillips)*.

One fact seems obvious in these various translations of the original Greek. Apparently the prophets were called to endure suffering and this lasted a long time. They have set a notable example of sticking to their testimony in their witness and in their ministry all through their suffering. The word "patience" in this case does not so much emphasize that they endured physical suffering, but that they kept on with their ministry in spite of the physical suffering. James urges upon Christians that they should look at the prophets and follow their example.

The first example James considers is the case of Moses. Moses went before Pharaoh and asked him to allow the children of Israel to come out of the land of Egypt. Pharaoh put off Moses time and time again. He would promise to let God's people go, and then he would change his mind. He disappointed Moses over and over again. Moses is a great example of steadfastness and constancy. He never wavered in his request.

Pharaoh made compromise offers, but Moses never changed his request for a three day journey into the wilderness that Israel might worship the Lord. Pharaoh suggested that they worship God in Egypt. Moses refused. Next Pharaoh said, "If you must go, go just a short distance." When Moses refused again, Pharaoh suggested that such a trip into the wilderness would be too hard for the little children. "Leave the little children here and then the rest of you can go." Moses said, "No, the little children belong to us; all of us will have to go three days journey into the wilderness." Finally Pharaoh said to Moses, "Take all the people but leave your flocks and herds here." Moses remained firm. In spite of the compromise offers, in spite of the prolonged suffering of the people, Moses was steadfast all the way through. This is an example for us. When we have once committed ourselves to the Lord let us never compromise, let us stay with our intention to serve Him all the way through.

When the children of Israel turned against him and murmured and complained Moses never gave up his God-given task. His task was to lead the people of Israel to the promised land and this he was going to do. When we think of Moses dealing with Israel we are reminded of a parent handling a rebellious child. We have watched a mother holding a little boy who starts kicking and screaming and hitting around with his hands and fists. Even when he kicks his feet against her she does not fight him. She just quietly takes hold of him and brings him through to what she has in mind. She stays patiently with him in spite of the way he is acting. That's the way it was with Moses.

This is the example of the prophet in "patience." By the grace of God Moses set an example in steadfastness when defeatism was all around him. When the people were ready to quit, when they threatened Moses, the man of God, and actually said that they should have stayed in Egypt and died there, he did not falter. Moses has set an example for us to follow. When once we start in the way of God we must keep right on in spite of any circumstances that seem to hinder us.

In connection with this thought we are often reminded of a ship at sea. When a ship is set to sail to the northeast, it will go northeast. The winds may blow from the west or the south or from the north. The waves may run high in an opposite direction, but that ship never varies from the way the compass points. It will hold its course all the way through. This is what James is telling Christians to do.

There are great examples of patience in the face of persecution and suffering in men of God, like Elijah and Elisha. These men at times had to flee for their lives. They had to act like fugitives, but they stayed with their task all the way through and never faltered. When Micaiah the prophet was brought before King Jehoshaphat to prophesy good things concerning the proposed military venture between Judah and Israel, Micaiah refused to predict victory when the Lord had shown him that the battle would end in disaster. Ahab the King of Israel was so angry because of Micaiah's prophecy of defeat that he ordered the prophet to be thrown into prison and to be fed with the bread and water "of affliction."

The prophet Jeremiah told the warning words of God to his king. He told the king over and over again what God wanted him to do. The king became so angry that he had the prophet of God thrown into a dungeon that was filled with mire. Jeremiah had sunk into the mire until it came up to his armpits when Ebed-melech, a servant of the king who feared God, came with thirty men and pulled the prophet to safety with a rope. This is the way in which that famous prophet was treated. One might ask, "How could such a thing happen? Wasn't this man in the will of the Lord?" He certainly was but this is how things can happen in this world.

We have been considering the prophets, but even Christians who live ordinarily lives may have troubles when they do what God would have them to do. How can this be? "A servant is not greater than his master" (John 15:20, *Amplified*). The Lord Jesus "came unto his own, and his own received him not" (John 1:11). Christians may run into real opposition because they are doing the will of God. This is possible, but we have the prophets for an example of steadfastness and patience. James would say, "Stick with it all the way through." In view of their sufferings ours are but slight. "Take, my brethren, the prophets, who have spoken in the name of the Lord, for an example of suffering affliction, and of patience."

Chapter 45

THE PATIENCE OF JOB

> Behold, we count them happy which endure. Ye have heard
> of the patience of Job, and have seen the end of the Lord; that
> the Lord is very pitiful, and of tender mercy (James 5:11).

"Behold, we count them happy which endure." To illustrate
the common truth of these words let us consider baseball. When
playing baseball it does not matter how fast we run from home
to first base. It does not matter how fast we run to second or to
third base. In order to score, we must run from third base to
home, and we must touch homeplate. That is, we have to complete the deal! It is the same with cooking. If we want a perfect
cake we must leave it in the oven the full time. The same thing
holds true with everything we do. It is the man who runs to the
finish line who wins the prize in the race. Now and again we
have watched competition of that sort. We have seen someone
do very well almost to the last moment and then let go and
give up. If we stop before the finish there is no score, no benefit
from what we have done.

This is the way it is in life. James is emphasizing the fact that
we must keep going, we must continue all the way, if we would
receive the blessing of God. One might ask, "What would hold us
back, what would hinder us from completing what we are doing?"
There are various things: we could become tired and quit for
that reason. We could be unstable. James had in mind that
Christians might be fickle and double-minded, at one time this
way and at another time that way. One who is this unstable
won't get anywhere. Earlier in this epistle James pointed out,
"Let not that man think that he shall receive any thing of the
Lord" (James 1:7). Now near the close of his letter James sums

up his teaching and emphasizes these things. "We count them happy which endure." He does not mean that when something happens that hurts us we are to count ourselves happy. He is not saying that when we suffer we are to count ourselves happy. James means to say when we keep trusting in spite of suffering, when we are faithful, in spite of distress, then we endure. To "endure" means going all the way to the finish. In this letter he is emphasizing that blessing is for those who "endure," not so much for those who suffer nor for those who have difficulties, but for those who persevere in spite of the suffering and in spite of the difficulties.

Some of us have experienced trouble when we have tried to do the right thing. There is always that temptation to quit because of the trouble. James would say, "Don't quit because you have trouble. Blessed is the man that endureth temptation (trouble)" (James 1:12). This is the way it was with Job. When James says, "Ye have heard of the patience of Job," he does not mean that Job took his sufferings comfortably and easily. Job didn't. As a matter of fact Job was the kind of person who could say, "ouch" when he hurt, and he did! Job not only lost everything he had, but he lost his health. He was covered with boils from the sole of his foot to the crown of his head. There wasn't a spot on his body that was not infected. When this pain came to Job he felt it and he cried. What showed his "patience" was that he never let go of God.

The Bible records that in spite of all his pain and suffering Job "did not sin with his lips," (Job 2:10, *Amplified)* nor did he "charge God foolishly" (Job 1:22). He kept his integrity. His faith and his confidence was in God, and he continued to believe even though he suffered. His wife told him that, suffering as he did, he should curse God and die. Job turned on her and told her that she talked like a foolish woman. Then he went on to say, "Shall we receive favor from the Lord and not receive distress? Should everything be going our way and nothing be going against us? If we receive blessing from God, and thank Him for the good, let us thank Him for the evil too. Let's thank Him for everything." This was Job's attitude. He was not about to quit. The patient person who stays with it to the finish gets results.

"And have seen the end of the Lord" means that you have seen in the record of Job that God will bring things to pass: you have seen what God eventually will do. In the case of Job everything turned out well. He had more at the end than he had in the beginning. God restored and multiplied everything he'd had before. James goes on to say, "The Lord is very pitiful, and of tender mercy." These words do not imply that if I lose a dollar God will give me two dollars. Nowhere in the Bible is there such a promise. The underlying idea seems rather to be that when I think I am following in God's way and lose five dollars I could consider that five dollars was given in the service of the Lord, and He will reward me. When I am mistreated because I am doing the will of God, I endure it. That's all there is to it. If I walk with the Lord, and if walking with Him leads me into trouble, trouble it is, and that's that. But God does more. This is what James is talking about. "Ye have heard of the patience of Job" — he stayed with his trust in God all the way through; "and have seen the end of the Lord" — the way in which God turned things around so that Job was benefited and blessed.

Once when the Lord Jesus talked to His disciples He told them that a man would have to give things up to follow Him. When He spoke of the rich He said, "It would be as hard for a rich man to enter into the kingdom of heaven, as it would be for a camel to go through the eye of a needle." (paraphrase of Matthew 19:24). To a person with assets and wealth, there is real difficulty in following the Lord. To follow Christ would mean giving up so much. Peter, speaking for the disciples, said to Him, "Master, we have forsaken all and have followed Thee, what do we have henceforth?" (paraphrase of Matthew 19:27). Peter was not showing unnatural interest. He just wanted to know what the situation would actually hold for him. The Lord told Peter, "There isn't anybody who forsakes houses and lands and father and mother and brothers and sisters, for My sake, and the Gospel, but will in this world receive an hundred fold, and in the world to come, everlasting life" (paraphrase of Matthew 19:28, 29). God will take care of His own in the way that is best for them.

Chapter 46

REMEMBER GOD AT ALL TIMES

> But above all things, my brethren, swear not, neither by
> heaven, neither by the earth, neither by any other oath: but
> let your yea be yea; and your nay, nay; lest ye fall into con-
> demnation. Is any among you afflicted? let him pray. Is any
> merry? let him sing psalms (James 5:12, 13).

Throughout his epistle, James has stressed the importance of
fruitful Christian living. He has emphasized and specified various things that will bring blessing into the lives of Christians.
Now toward the end of his letter he draws attention to human
weakness, and to our tendency to seek for help outside God.

What does James mean by the words in this passage? What
is he telling us? Actually, James knows that when we feel a
special need, when we are up against it, we look for help. There
is always a temptation to try to manipulate things, to scheme
and figure out some way to get out of trouble by ourselves.
We'd move heaven and earth, so to speak, if that were possible.
James would say, "If you're in trouble, brother, ask for help: do
not pretend you don't need it. Don't go reaching out to the
heavens to try and bring something down. Don't go looking
around on earth to try and find something. If you're in trouble,
turn to God."

It is our human tendency, first of all to pretend that everything
is going just wonderfully. Though it's probably not the case, we
try to make it seem that way. We are so anxious to evade
clear-cut observation and analysis. We hate to admit that sometimes we feel so badly about ourselves that we wish we could
hide. Many of us do feel that way, and in our desire to escape

notice we hide behind things and then look for help from outside the situation in which we find ourselves. Perhaps we look for help from the heavens, hoping somehow in providence. Some people will just say, "I hope I will get lucky." They have the idea in mind that in some way the stars will work things out. James would say, "Don't do it! Admit the truth of the situation as it is. Turn to God!"

When James says, "Don't swear by heaven; don't swear by the earth," he means don't depend on some fortunate circumstance like a good day when the sun shines and everything is just fine. We may search for some way of managing by clever tricks. We want to work out some solution so that we can win. Sometimes we look around for a smart idea. We would like to find some clever way to do things so that we could handle it ourselves. James would say, "That's looking to the things of earth for your help." It is as if we were taking an oath — committing ourselves to it. We have heard the ejaculation, "Well, heaven help me." That's the general idea implied by the word "swear," as James uses it.

"Neither by any other oath." Many people will go to sooth-sayers and to fortune tellers. They will wear certain charms, or do things in a certain way. Not so long ago someone asked me to explain how the ouija board works. Then I was shown the crystal ball idea of finding out things. It is surprising how many people go by these gadgets, by these charms, by some form of magic. We do not give all this a public status by publicizing it in the newspapers, but we may be amazed by the number of folks who follow astrology. The news stands are featuring a great variety of books on the stars, on astrology, and all related subjects. James is warning us this is the wrong way to seek help when we are in difficulties, when we are in a predicament. Looking for help in this way could lead us into condemnation.

"Above all things, my brethren, swear not." That means, don't count on help, "neither by heaven, neither by the earth, neither by any other oath: but let your yea, be yea; and your nay, nay." Play it straight the way it is, just admit all things as they are, "lest ye fall into condemnation." There are many people who will carry a lucky penny or a rabbit's foot in their pockets. They wear charms around their necks and hang them in their cars to ward off bad luck. They actually trust in these things. This is more serious than we might realize. Once in a while we read of some man of wealth or culture who has been "taken in" by fortune tellers, by clairvoyance, and such like. We never hear of the many others who have had similar experiences.

The Bible brings us to the revelation of God. It says to all who will listen, "Put away all those subtle magic ways of getting things done. Play it in the open, in broad daylight." "Let your yea, be yea, and your nay, nay." We may say, "But we are in distress." James will tell us what to do. In the very next verse we read, "Is any among you afflicted" (if you're in trouble) "let him pray." Now there we are! We need no charms, we need not fear a black cat running across our path. We need not worry about walking under a ladder, nor figure that number 13 is unlucky. "Is any among you afflicted?" Are you having real trouble? "Let him pray." "Is any merry?" Are you fortunate? Is everything going your way? Are you having a wonderful time? "Let him sing psalms." Praise God. Thank God. If you are in trouble, trust God. If you're having wonderful success, thank God. In all things and at all times keep God in the picture.

Each of us should thank God for a man like James, who wrote this warning for us to see. We can take his words with us as far as our whole life in concerned. We need not go around looking for some magic. We don't need it. We need not find out whether the astrological chart or guide in the newspaper is going to guide us. We can look up to God. We can pray when in trouble, we can praise Him when all goes well. We have a wonderful God!

Chapter 47

PRAYER FOR THE SICK

> Is any sick among you? let him call for the elders of the
> church; and let them pray over him, anointing him with oil in
> the name of the Lord (James 5:14).

Being sick is a common experience. No one lives very long
without being sick at some time or another. No one likes to be
sick. One thing is certain, when we are sick we need help.
Now it is a natural thing for a Christian when he really needs
help to turn to God, anywhere, any time. He feels that God has
the power and is able to help. Any man with confidence in God
naturally will turn to Him for help. And it is true God can help
any man and He should be asked to help.

Reading the words of our Scripture passage arouses a sense of
loss and pity. Most members in the large denominations seem
to have neglected the promises about God answering such
prayers. I was not born a Christian. I was born a Canadian, and
I grew to manhood before I became a believer. Believing the
Gospel of the Lord Jesus Christ was the most astonishing thing
that ever happened in my life. I had never experienced anything
like it before. When I became a Christian I believed that God
was a living God: that He was Almighty and really could help.
I attended services in a historic, well-known denomination, but
I did not hear anyone talk about getting answers to prayer.

In my home town church which I attended before I became
a Christian, we never talked about prayer. The preacher prayed.
The people who conducted Sunday school prayed. There was
always prayer said in the church services. In these public prayers
men seemed to ask for everything, but I noticed that when there

was trouble in the community or trouble in some family no one thought about asking God for help. When I became a Christian, I felt saddened to think that church people everywhere seemed not to know that God will hear and answer prayer.

We can get help from God! James 5:14 gives us sufficient authority to pray to God anywhere, in any church and in any denomination. There is not a church that is named by the name of the Lord Jesus Christ that could not take this verse and live by it. "Is any sick among you? let him call for the elders of the church; and let them pray over him, anointing him with oil in the name of the Lord." What would be wrong with that? Why don't we do it?

The word "sick" simply means that the body of a person who is ill does not function properly because the normal activities are impeded. If any one of our organs is not acting right, if any part of our body is not functioning properly, then we are sick. If there are in our bodies certain microbes or disease germs or foreign bodies, our vitality will be affected.

Besides physical illnesses a person may be mentally sick. Such persons are beset by abnormal fears. All their thinking is wrong. They may feel abused and ridiculed and persecuted. There are also people who are emotionally ill. Such are easily confused and flustered. They are ready to become angry at the mention of something they don't like. When they hate a neighbor they become almost ill when they see him. These are emotionally disturbed. Then there are the people who are intellectually sick. This is the group which is most difficult to help. They have ideologies that are all confused because they are based on wrong ideas. So the word "sick" does not only apply to those who are physically ill.

There is no reason why we should limit it to physical illness here. "Is there any sick among you?" (anybody who is not functioning properly) "let him call for the elders of the church." Now who would such men be? The elders of any church would be men of faith, men of responsibility, men of authority. Because they are Christians they feel responsibility for others, and can be trusted. They have been elected and can speak for the church as a whole. They are men who really do believe in God.

When such a group of believing Christians come together,

some are stronger in their faith than others. James would tell us to bring together the people who have the closest relationship with God. "And let them pray over him, anointing him with oil in the name of the Lord."

Sometimes this is done by elders as they gather around the sick. They anoint him with oil and pray for him. But James has more to say about this procedure: all is to be done "in the name of the Lord."

This anointing is always associated with the Holy Spirit. It means bringing the Holy Spirit into the life of that person. James had in mind that if the elders would gather together and pray for this sick man, they could actually by their faith in the Lord bring the Holy Spirit to bear upon him. I feel no objection to the use of oil. They can use olive oil or anything else they want to! But we need to go deeper than that: it is not the oil that will do it. It is the power of the Holy Spirit brought to bear in the name of the Lord.

"In the name of the Lord" is one of the most significant phrases in the New Testament. It means doing whatever is being done while trusting in the Lord Jesus Christ for everything He has promised. It means acting with faith in the Lord Jesus Christ, who came to die for our sins, who died to be raised from the dead and to ascend into heaven, who is even now praying for all believers. Faith in Him and faith in His power is the dynamic in all actions of faith. When the Lord was here He said that whatever He did His followers would be able to do. To perform in this fashion we must come with faith in God's power and His purpose.

The important lesson in this portion of the Scripture is to have believers bring the sick person to the Lord for His blessing.

Chapter 48

BELIEVING PRAYER WILL ACCOMPLISH

> And the prayer of faith shall save the sick, and the Lord shall raise him up; and if he have committed sins, they shall be forgiven him (James 5:15).

Perhaps this verse does not have its real significance with many because we have made it mean something more and something different than it actually means. If a Christian is going to exercise himself in praying "the prayer of faith" he must find some promise of God that will apply to the situation that he is facing. Praying the prayer of faith is not a function of self-will. We are not making up our minds to do something. This is out of our hands, this is something God will do. The prayer of faith means first to know God's promises, then to believe His promise about this particular thing. When we spend time with Him and seek His mind, we will know how to pray.

"The prayer of faith shall save the sick." We look at the word "save" and ask, "Do you mean heal?" It may mean "heal" but this is not limited to the physical. Actually the word "save" is very close to the word "heal." Those of us who are acquainted with the German language know that Luther translated the word salvation as "Heilung" which is the German word for "healing." When Luther spoke of the Lord Jesus Christ as his Saviour he used the word, "Heiland," which is derived from the German word "heal." This is how Luther understood salvation. So we may say that the words "shall save the sick" may also mean "heal the sick," but does not necessarily limit this to the physical. We recall that there are various kinds of sicknesses: the physical, the mental, the emotional and the intellectual. In any one of these

God will restore that part to normal function which needs His healing touch. In any one of these sicknesses "the prayer of faith" shall save the sick.

When the elders, the strong in faith gather around the sick person, they anoint him in the name of the Lord. They bring the Holy Spirit to the sick brother, anointing him in the name of the Lord. "The Lord shall raise Him up." Why should we limit this promise to the healing of the body? "Raise him up" is the language we use for the resurrection. It is bringing him into the newness of life. If we want to consider the wider con-text of this we must look ahead to verses 16, 17, 18, 19 and 20, and see what James is discussing in this context.

James is recognizing that some believers, as they live with the Lord, may become sick or may become unbalanced. This can be in the spirit, it can be in the mind, in the emotions, and it can be in the body. No Christian could have an objection to that. There is such a thing as bodily healing, but let us not limit healing to that. "And if he have committed sins, they shall be forgiven him." As far as the responsibility for our sins is concerned, and as far as our being sinners in the sight of God is concerned, all this shall be forgiven to us when we turn to God in faith. This does not mean that our sins will not have consequences. For instance, suppose a believer has done some-thing foolish that resulted in the amputation of his leg. When the elders of the church gather around him and pray for him, he may be forgiven for his foolish conduct but his leg is not going to be restored. In discussing these serious things we should be realistic and avoid loose talk about these things, which could inspire vain hope.

Sometimes a verse like this is taken to mean so many things that it finally comes to mean nothing. For example, if verse 14 referred to the physical healing only, no Christian need die. In that case every funeral in any church would mean that the elders in that church had failed. If we take that verse to mean that if the elders exercised their faith the sick would get well, then believers could look forward to living here forever. This is simply not true. We know there are good people with real faith in God who have died young.

If a man has spiritual problems: if he has in himself hatred for his fellow man he needs healing. If a man has in himself doubt, if there is envy of some church members and malice toward others, this man needs healing. The elders should be praying for such a person. This would really help.

The problems which call for prayer could include physical illness, but we can be assured that James had a much broader idea in mind when he presented this truth. We can be sure that James did not expect people to go on living in this world forever.

Rather James would stress the truth that anyone can be forgiven. Everyone and anyone can be forgiven. This is what he wanted believers to have in mind. He wanted them to remember that if they would bring the sick person to the Lord and pray for him the Lord would bless that sick person. If the sickness was due to some sin the sin would be forgiven. There may be more in this verse which we do not fully understand, but the Lord will help us. One thing is sure and certain, we should at all times turn to the Lord in prayer that His will should be done.

Chapter 49

PRAY FOR ONE ANOTHER

> Confess your faults one to another, and pray one for another, that ye may be healed. The effectual fervent prayer of a righteous man availeth much (James 5:16).

In our meditation on the previous verse, "the prayer of faith," we felt that James had much more in mind than the continuation of physical life. He had our relationship with God and holy living in mind. This is the way he writes to believers and Christians. When James says, "Confess your faults," the word "confess" would mean that we would admit our faults. We will acknowledge them to one another. We will describe the things that are not as they should be. We are to do this only in order to receive the blessing of intercessory prayer. We do not confess because we are trying to atone for something we have done. We do not do this in any sadistic way. We share with each other the things in ourselves that are not as they ought to be, because we want help. Many of us would be spiritually greatly blessed if we would say to one another what it is about ourselves that is not what it ought to be. We would be helped if we would admit what it is about ourselves and about our way of doing things that is wrong. Many believers have been helped by putting their faults into words. Then let us confess our faults that others may join in prayer for us.

When we speak of faults we refer to the characteristics in us that hinder us in serving the Lord. It may even mean sins. This word "faults" has been translated as sins when we acknowledge the things in us which are not like the Lord Jesus Christ. They are faults of that nature. They would not necessarily be psychological, or intellectual, or mental faults, but faults of the spirit. When we are selfish, proud or jealous of other people, all these would be faults. "Confess your faults one to another" — traits in us that actually hinder blessing. This promise is not for everyone, but for us who believe in the Lord Jesus Christ. We can confess to one another because the people we talk to know that God is going to be on our side when we do.

"And pray one for another." We will be able to pray intelligently when we have heard what the problem is. And so we pray one for another. It is so important to be specific about what we are going to pray for in order to get an answer to our prayers. There are many people who do not receive answers to their prayers because they never ask specifically for anything. We may for instance pray, "Lord, bless our family." How would we know if God blessed our family? But now suppose we have a boy who can't apply himself at school, and doesn't attend to his home work. So we pray. "Oh Lord, bless Jim, and help him to attend to his work and to get his homework done." We'd pray in this way, and it turns out that in the next week, Jim actually does his work better. This would be our blessing.

Suppose in a family there are two girls who quarrel. They argue with each other and pick on each other, and this troubles others. The parents scold them but that doesn't seem to help. So they turn to the Lord and ask Him to bless them. How will this blessing appear? One of the two girls will no longer argue. That is all it would take to stop the quarreling, really. One of the girls doesn't want to fuss any more or maybe both of them. This is what was prayed for.

Perhaps some of us have members in our family who become ill easily. We hope they will get through the winter without the usual illness. We pray about this, and we ask the Lord to bless us. This would be a proper prayer. Praying specifically we can then experience God's specific answer to our prayers.

Often when we pray, "God will bless our family," we cannot really know whether He did or not. It is when we ask for Jim and his school work, and for Mary and Jane not to argue so much, when we become specific, that we know whether our prayers were answered. These examples are by way of explaining how important specific prayer is. Let us ask in a specific, candid, honest way that we may be healed of whatever fault besets us. This is what we are asked to do. Then follows this remarkable sentence: "The effectual fervent prayer of a righteous man availeth much."

Who is a righteous man? It would be easy to say that he is someone who is perfect. But since there is no one who is perfect, how can a man be righteous? A man cannot become righteous living by himself. He can only be righteous if his attitude toward God is right. When his attitude toward God is right his conduct will be good. This does not imply that he is righteous because of his good conduct. Rather, it is because he trusts in the Lord Jesus Christ and believes in Him as his Saviour: he rests his soul in faith in the Lord Jesus Christ and in His righteousness. This faith makes a man righteous in the sight of God.

When we are right with God we will pray to Him. When we are right with God we will read the Bible. When we are right with God we will go to church to worship God. We will invite others to church. Then as we implement our faith in actual conduct, we will pray the effectual, fervent prayer of faith. "Effectual" prayer will be practical prayer. We will actually look for and work for effect in prayer. Praying for specific things, praying fervently and earnestly to God for help, this kind of prayer availeth much.

Another translation of this verse reads thus: "Confess to one another therefore your faults — your slips, your false steps, your offenses, your sins; and pray [also] for one another, that you may be healed and restored — to a spiritual tone of mind and heart. The earnest (heartfelt, continued) prayer of a righteous man makes tremendous power available — dynamic in its working." *(Amplified)*

Another translator puts it in these words, "Therefore confess your sins to one another, and pray for one another, and then you will be healed. A good man's prayer is powerful and effective" *(New English Bible)*. Another translation reads as follows, "Therefore, confess your sins to one another, and pray for one another, so that you will be healed. The prayer of a righteous man has a powerful effect" *(Today's English Version)*. Here is another version of the same verse, "You should get into the habit of admitting your sins to each other, and praying for each other, so that if sickness comes to you you may be healed. Tremendous power is made available through a good man's earnest prayer" *(Phillips)*. These various translations express the same truth. May we avail ourselves of the power which is available in fervent, earnest prayer.

Chapter 50

THE PRAYER OF A BELIEVING MAN

> Elijah was a man subject to like passions as we are, and he
> prayed earnestly that it might not rain: and it rained not on
> the earth by the space of three years and six months. And he
> prayed again, and the heaven gave rain, and the earth brought
> forth her fruit. Brethren, if any of you do err from the truth,
> and one convert him; let him know, that he which converteth
> the sinner from the error of his way, shall save a soul from
> death, and shall hide a multitude of sins (James 5:17-20).

What a wonderful book this book of James has been. How
much practical truth it contains for all of us. In the last verses
of his book, James speaks to us who are believers, on the power
of prayer. This prophet Elijah, whose name in Greek is Elias,
was a mighty man of prayer. James points out for us that Elijah
was just a man. He was not a common man but he was of like
passions as we are.

Another translation helps us get the overall picture: "Elijah was
a human being with a nature as we have — with feelings, affections and constitution as ourselves; and he prayed earnestly for
it not to rain, and no rain fell on the earth for three years and
six months. And [then] he prayed again, and "the heavens supplied rain and the land produced its crop [as usual]" (James 5:
17, 18, *Amplified*). The thing for us to realize is that praying is
not by our power, it is not by the power of any man. Elijah
was not an angel. He was not an archangel. He was a human
being and from this we are to understand that the power of
Elijah's prayer was not in Elijah. It was in God.

Another translation emphasizes the same thought: "Elijah was
a man with human frailties like our own; and when he prayed

earnestly that there should be no rain, not a drop fell on the land for three years and a half; then he prayed again, and down came the rain and the land bore crops once more" (James 5:17, 18, *New English Bible*). Elijah prayed about rain. James is telling us to pray for one another, about our faults and our needs. In another translation we read, "Elijah was the same kind of person we are" (James 5:17, *Today's English Version*). This is to encourage us to pray. Hearing about Elijah we may think in our hearts what a wonderful thing it is that God answered Elijah's prayer. What a wonderful thing prayer is! And that is true.

Have we ever considered how wonderful it is that whether we are in our own home or in our office we can pray? We too could be receiving the power of God through prayer. How we should desire to have this power of prayer in our home! Praying is not something we get out and push. It's not something we get out and pull. This power of prayer is something we reach up and receive.

Whatever we may be facing on any day, let us look up to God. Let us reach up to receive His promise and His power. We have read that Elijah prayed for rain, but we have read in verse 16 about praying for one another. In the last two verses of this wonderful book James tells us how we may receive an added blessing. "Brethren, if any of you err from the truth," (in the faults we read about in verse 16), "and one convert him;" (possibly through the prayer of someone who cares for him,) "Let him know, that he which converteth the sinner from the error of his way" (not the unregenerate sinner who has never heard of Christ, but the Christian who is doing wrong): if one convert him "from the error of his way, shall save a soul from death, and shall hide a multitude of sins."

In another translation it is expressed thus: "[My] brethren, if anyone among you strays from the Truth and falls into error, and another [person] brings him back [to God], let the [latter] one be sure that whoever turns a sinner from his evil course will save [that one's] soul from death and will cover a multitude of sins [that is, procure the pardon of the many sins committed by the convert]" (James 5:19, 20, *Amplified*). Another version of the same Scripture is, "My brothers! If one of you wanders away from the truth, and another one brings him back again, remember this: whoever turns a sinner back from his wrong ways will save that sinner's soul from death, and cause a great number of sins to be forgiven" (James 5:19, 20, *Today's English Version*). Isn't it wonderful to think that we could do this by praying?

Only God knows every individual life. Only God knows our problems. There are some things we do not understand or know. But there is one thing of which we can be absolutely sure. Whatever our problems, whatever our situation or circumstance, we can know that God answers prayer.

Another version of these verses is, "My brothers, if one of your number should stray from the truth and another succeed in bringing him back, be sure of this: any man who brings a sinner back from his crooked ways will be rescuing his soul from death and cancelling innumerable sins" (James 5:19, 20, *New English Bible*). Isn't this a wonderful thought? James wants us to notice the way others are doing, to talk to one another about the problems and to encourage each other. He would have us confess our faults to one another because we have a powerful God to whom we can turn for help in every situation.

Another translator writes, "My brothers, if any of you should wander away from the truth and another should turn him back onto the right path, then the latter may be sure that in turning a man back from his wandering course he has rescued a soul from death, and his loving action will 'cover a multitude of sins'" (James 5:19, 20, *Phillips*). Isn't this remarkable? When we see one another in trouble, or see one of our number overtaken by a fault, James wants us to call upon God and to pray for one another. This is confirmed by what we read in I John 5:16. Here we find John saying that we ought to pray for the brother who has done wrong and he will be forgiven. These are John's words, "If any man see his brother sin a sin which is not unto death, he shall ask, and he shall give him life for them that sin not unto death." John would have us pray for our brother's forgiveness also, but James would have us pray with him for his deliverance.

This book of James has been like a gardener's manual, a book showing us how we can actually accomplish living in the will of God. Throughout his book, James has been practical: he has been realistic. He has not gone into any high and mighty ways of saying things. His words have been carefully chosen. They have been direct, simple and plain. They have expressed his sure belief that God can help us. If we walk in His way, if we play it straight, if we turn to God, if we believe in God, if we pray to God and we work with God He will surely bless us.